Contemporary Basque Fiction

BOOKS IN THE BASQUE SERIES

THE BASQUE SERIES

CONTEMPORARY

Basque Fiction

AN ANTHOLOGY

INTRODUCTION AND COMMENTARY BY

JESÚS MARÍA LASAGABASTER

Translated by Michael E. Morris

University of Nevada Press : Reno & Las Vegas

Basque Series Editor: William A. Douglass

The paper used in this book meets the requirements of American National Standard for Information Sciences—Permanence of Paper for Printed Library Materials, ANSI Z39.48-1984. Binding materials were chosen for strength and durability.

University of Nevada Press, Reno, Nevada 89557 USA

Printed in the United States of America
Design by Richard Hendel

Library of Congress Cataloging-in-Publication Data

Antología de la narrativa vasca actual. English
Contemporary Basque fiction : an anthology / introduction and commentary by Jesús María Lasagabaster ; translated by Michael E. Morris.
p. cm. – (The Basque series)
Translation of: Antología de la narrativa vasca actual.
ISBN 0-87417-158-X (alk. paper)
1. Short stories, Basque–Translations into English. 2. Short stories, English–Translations from Basque. I. Lasagabaster Madinabeitia, Jesús María, 1931– . II. Series.
PH5397.E8A58 1990
899'.9230108'09045–dc20
90-11921
CIP

2 4 6 8 9 7 5 3 1

The stories in this volume appeared first in Basque in a variety of books and periodicals and were then published in Spanish translation in *Antología de la narrativa Vasca actual,* edited by Jesús María Lasagabaster (Barcelona, Spain: Edicions del Mall, 1986; copyright © 1986 by Euskal Idazleen Elkartea). Used here by permission of Euskal Idazleen Elkartea, the Basque Writers' Association. Translation from Basque to English was funded by a grant from Euskal Idazleen Elkartea.

Contents

Preface

It would seem appropriate to explain the criteria used in selecting the following texts. The intention was to choose complete works, or at least those substantial enough to be intelligible outside their literary whole. Short stories have been chosen whenever possible. In the case of excerpts from novels, the preference has been to choose whole chapters.

The criterion of literary quality, decisive in such an anthology as this, has been applied jointly with other secondary, but equally decisive, factors in choosing the texts. We believe that, within the obvious limits of this book, the works presented here are representative of modern Basque narrative. Within this sample we see two emphases: First, there is the history and evolution of Basque prose written in the last twenty-five years. Second, there is the sociocultural and linguistic-literary trends that are taking place now, and which are determining not only the current style of the prose but its future orientation as well.

Jesús María Lasagabaster
Professor of Literature at Estudios
Universitarios y Técnicos de Guipúzcoa
Donostia (San Sebastián)

Introduction

The Basque narrative has been with us for scarcely one hundred years and has followed a long and winding path within that short period. Basque narrative prose, like that of other literatures, grew out of works which were not literary in the strictest contemporary sense of the word; that is, works which do not fall easily into traditional literary genres.

Spanish prose developed from the efforts of Alfonso "the Wise" and the Toledo School of Translators through the use of Spanish in judicial and historical works such as *Las partidas* and *Grande e general estoria*. In the case of Basque, works of an aesthetic and religious nature served as the foundation of its literary prose. Examples include Leizarraga and his sixteenth-century translation of the Bible; Pedro de Axular and his classic, *Gero*; Cardaveraz in the seventeenth century; and the works of Mendiburu in the eighteenth. But there were certain characteristics specific to the birth of Basque literature and narrative prose, setting them apart from their Spanish and French counterparts.

First, the development of the early aesthetic prose into narrative was a very slow process. It was not until the nineteenth century that the first examples of modern Basque narrative came into being. In 1800, Juan Antonio de Moguel wrote his book *Peru Abarka* (Peter Brogue) which was a collection of dialogues written in a minimally literary style. The work had a markedly didactic and apologetic goal. Although a critic might have considered *Peru Abarka* the first Basque-language novel, it was not until the late nineteenth century that we find works written explicitly according to narrative conventions. Apart from an occasional short story, originally written in French and translated into Basque, the first Basque-language novel in the strictest sense appeared in 1898. This was the work *Auñemendiko lorea* (The Flower of the Pyrenees) whose author, Txomin Agirre, later gave birth to the Basque "costumbrista" novel, or novel of manners. *Auñemendiko lorea* is a historical-romantic work that was strongly influenced by Navarro Villoslada's

Amaya. The fact that the novel itself was slow to be recognized as a separate literary genre (Hegel believed it to be the epic of modern bourgeois society) is accentuated in the case of the Basque novel.

A second characteristic of the slow development and formation of Basque narrative was the fact that between Leizarraga and Txomin Agirre—or, to be more precise, between Leizarraga and Moguel—from the sixteenth through the nineteenth centuries, the body of Basque literature was composed of little more than aesthetic writings, catechisms, books on meditation, and collections of sermons. To be sure, Axular has his place in the history of Basque literature in the same dignified and venerated way as, for example, Fray Luis de Granada and Bossuet have their places in Spanish and French literature. However, that which sets Basque literature apart is that all authors were like Axular; that is, all wrote aesthetic and religious books exclusively.

Between 1545—the date of the first literary creation written in Basque—and 1879, 102 books were printed in the language. Of this total, only 4 were literary in the modern sense. All the rest were books on language and, above all, on religious topics. For this reason we make the general statement that the slow development hitherto attributed to the Basque novel is characteristic of all literature written in this language. Indeed, Basque literary tradition has been essentially oral. Oral Basque literature, as Koldo Mitxelena correctly points out, is quantitatively abundant and qualitatively comparable to that of any other culture. Written literature, on the other hand, was produced only sporadically from the sixteenth century on, and then more for linguistic or religious reasons than for literary ones. The institutionalization of written literature as a specific cultural practice within the social fabric began in the middle of the nineteenth century with poetry competitions (*lore jokuak*) and periodicals, but these developments were not consolidated until well into the twentieth.

Thus, in order to describe the phenomenon of Basque literature (that is, written literature), it is necessary to understand this oral literary tradition, which is varied in both content and modes of expression and of high quality as well. This opposition of traditional oral versus written literature can be explained, for example, by the development of cultured poetry which preceded narrative prose by several centuries. Until now, verse (written and oral) has taken precedence over prose in terms of both quantity and quality.

The novel is a genre which has no roots in Basque literary tradition.

It first surfaced between the nineteenth and twentieth centuries as a means more suitable than poetry for promoting the Basque language. It was a product of the political-cultural movement which sprang up in the Basque Country towards the latter third of the nineteenth century after the Second Carlist War. The novel was thus born as an effective vehicle for promoting and teaching the language, since the existence of novels helps to generate a new reading public. Indeed, the first Basque novels by Txomin Agirre and Etxeita were called *irakurgayak* or "readings" by their authors.

In contrast with the lector of previous centuries, who either read the aesthetic books of Axular or Cardaveraz or heard them read in churches, the new Basque reader is, or portends to be, a consumer of "lay" literature which does not speak to his or her religious needs. Rather, paradoxically, it appeals to a "disinterested" need for entertainment, as well as for learning and practicing Basque. Indeed, it is readily apparent that the Basque novel was subordinated to a certain linguistic purpose from the moment of inception. Even the first Basque poet, Bernard Etxepare, wrote with the intention of putting Basque on a par with the rest of the developed languages of the world. In his poem "*Kontrapas*" appeared the cry, "*Heuskara ialgi hadi kanpora*" (Basque, go forth), and it continued to be a rallying cry for the first Basque narrative writers almost four hundred years later.

It has even reached the point where the invaluable and beneficial service that Basque literature performed for its minority language, deprived of a place in higher cultural spheres, has been converted in practice to a kind of servitude that dissolves the undeniable individuality that every written literature should have into a linguistic end, destroying the autonomy of the literature that should extend beyond the language that serves it as both a support and vehicle of expression. The greatest service a writer can render his language is to renounce none of the purposes that constitute the nature and specific function of literature.

At any rate, the birth of narrative prose, and more specifically the novel, was an important step for Basque literature towards its identification and institutionalization within the cultural and social fabric of Basque society. And it is precisely the sociocultural context that has left a decisive mark on the stylistic and thematic orientation of the Basque novel from its inception to the second half of the twentieth century. Basque identity is founded on a system of values, the purpose of which, until the end of the nineteenth century, was political recovery and the spread of culture. At the center of the system we find the most important of those values, the Basque language.

When we speak of the areas where Basque has persisted, the areas where it has suffered less linguistic contamination, we usually mean the rural hinterland and coastal fishing villages. These serve as a paradigmatic and rustic model for a people who saw its national collective identity threatened after the loss of its *fueros* or "old laws." The literary form that corresponds to this value system was the costumbrista novel with its strong idealistic roots and obvious romantic flavor. This genre, set in a rural area or a fishing village, was not an invitation to reality but rather the product of an abstract, ideal model of reality that dominated literature and was served by it.

All the characteristics of the costumbrista novel, described by historians and literary sociologists as "statecraft," duality, orthodoxy, and absence of problems, are nakedly if not aggressively manifest in the Basque novel. When the novel—in more developed European literatures, already matured as a literary form of understanding reality through experiencing it—began to move in an avant-garde direction, the Basque novel was taking its first hesitant steps by adopting the organization of the universe of a novel and a vision of the world that the literatures of neighboring languages had already left behind. Well into the twentieth century, the Basque novel, in the majority of cases, complied with the stylistic, thematic, and ideological conventions of the novel of manners with strong romantic tones.

For this reason, if we began this introduction by alluding to that long and tortuous path along which the Basque narrative has traveled in the one hundred years of its existence, it is now imperative to point out that most of that trail was blazed in the past thirty years.

The Modernization of the Basque Narrative:
Txillardegi and Saizarbitoria

It is only in the second half of the twentieth century, namely the fifties and sixties, that Basque literature has entered the modern age. By this we mean two fundamental things: (1) the culmination of the institutionalization of literature, referring to poetry, which began in the second half of the nineteenth century; and (2) explicit or implicit reference to the great contemporary narratives rather than to traditional Basque literature. All in all, this means that the modernization of the Basque novel has historically been realized in terms of rupture: a break with the narrative, thematic, and ideological universes that sustained the costumbrista novel and with the worlds represented there; a break with its style and narrative technique; and finally, a departure from the very concept of literature as situated within a conscious and collective effort of cultural self-identification.

Regarding the contemporary history of Basque literature, it is unanimously agreed that José Luis Alvarez Emparanza (alias Txillardegi) and Ramón Saizarbitoria are the first pioneers of this current of change that has swept through Basque literature during the past twenty-five years. It is often said that the Basque novel owes its thematic modernization to Txillardegi and its incorporation of modern literary techniques to Saizarbitoria.

Even if all this is substantially true, raising such a complex question as the change in Basque narrative constitutes an overly simplistic approach, for it cannot be viewed as a simple break with earlier conventions of the literary comprehension and expression of reality. The contemporary Basque novel can only be properly understood with reference to a new system of values which ranges from politics to literature and finally to culture. Indeed, Txillardegi and Saizarbitoria were the first to express this sensitivity in their novels, just as Gabriel Aresti and Jon Mirande were the first to do so in poetry. But it is still risky to mechanically assign responsibilities and functions to individuals involved in the modernization process.

Txillardegi published his first novel, entitled *Leturiaren egunkari ezkutua* (Leturia's Secret Diary) in 1957. I myself have said and written on more than one occasion that Leturia is the first problematic hero of the Basque novel: an "antihero," the opposite of the unconditionally positive hero (individual or collective) of the earlier costumbrista novel, just as the "picaro" was the opposite of the wandering knight. However, the ancestors of Leturia's work are not Lázaro de Tormes or Guzmán de Alfarache, but rather Antoine de Roquentin from *La nausée* or the doubly "strange" Mersault from the novel *L'étranger*. Leturia—incredulous, desperate, and suicidal—is an unorthodox character representing a lucid negation of the stale ideological, moral, and even physical orthodoxy paradigmatically portrayed in the character Joanes, the patriarch and elderly shepherd prominently featured in the novel *Garoa* (Fern) which is one of the most typical and popular examples of the Basque costumbrista novel.

"*Ura zan gizona, ura!*" (What a man he was!) begins the admiring omniscient narrator of *Garoa*. He describes the seven-foot-tall protagonist as being as upright as a poplar, as wide around as the thickest beech tree, and as strong as an oak—all at the age of seventy-two. "*Bakarrik nago Zerubidean*" (I'm alone in Zerubide Park) begins the secret diary of the solitary protagonist in Txillardegi's novel. The unorthodox and melancholy Leturia did not have an admiring narrator to draw her out of her self-involvement in the quiet park of Zerubide and carry her through the pages of an honorable biography as did the shepherd Joanes, a king in his Aloña highlands, an ideal and a model for readers and Basques. Neither did the picaros of the Spanish baroque period have eulogists such as those who accompanied the wandering knights, praising their exploits. In the case of Leturia, as well as the picaros, we have nothing to go on but a secret diary brought to light by an audacious compiler. Leturia is almost fifty years younger than the shepherd Joanes, and her period of Basque history explains her modest but healthy heterodoxy —and even requires it.

The modernization of the Basque novel, like that of poetry during the 1960s, is part of a more universal project which is not only literary and cultural, but ideological and political as well: an alternative to the uniform monolithic system of collective identification and political recovery set into motion by the Basque Nationalist Party since its foundation at the end of the nineteenth century. In contrast with the ruralism of the earlier costumbrista works, the new Basque novel is the expression of an urban culture whose secular character and ideological pluralism have been recorded and accepted. It is this new way of seeing and interpreting Basque reality that requires young writers to seek a method just as new to express it literarily.

The costumbrista genre is no longer useful as a vision of the world or as a narrative technique. In his first novel, Txillardegi incorporates problems of an unmistakably existential nature into the Basque narrative. In order to do this, in line with a good many existential novelists, he uses the diary technique characterized by a self-reflecting, first-person narration. Historians of the modern Basque novel may not have sufficiently emphasized the strength and coherence employed by Txillardegi in resolving the problem of joining theme with viewpoint in his first novel. Perhaps this is due to the fact that both the reader and the critic thought it natural for the protagonist to tell the story that the author wished to relate by means of a secret diary in which her problematic existential journey is recorded in the natural rhythm of the seasons. Roquentin and Mersault had done it before, as had the enigmatic—and anonymous?—Jean Baptiste Clamence in Albert Camus's novel La chute (The Fall). But Leturia, as narrator of her own story, was also important because, perhaps unintentionally, she moved the Basque narrative toward a lyrical form of storytelling, in tune with a strong current within the contemporary novel and in contrast with the epic gentleness of the costumbrista novel.

In 1969, twelve years after Leturiaren egunkari ezkutua, Ramón Saizarbitoria's first novel, Egunero hasten delako (Because It Begins Every Day), confirmed that the modernization of the Basque novel had reached a point of no return. In Saizarbitoria's work, one can see even more clearly the author's conscious effort to find a new raison d'être for the Basque novel as both a representation of reality and as literature. His contribution to Basque narrative is an obvious and decisive enrichment of form and technique. Through Saizarbitoria's varied use of second-person narrative—dialogue in Egunero hasten delako, an inward-looking perspective in 100 metro (100 Meters), 1976—and his Beckett-like objectivism in the work Ene Jesus (My Jesus), 1976, the Basque novel irrevocably entered the modern age, plunging into the unchanneled current of a continuous and disconcerting search, not only for reality but also for literature.

In a brief prologue to Saizarbitoria's third novel, Koldo Izagirre notes that this novelist seems condemned to being a "man of firsts" ("lehen aldiko gizona") because he is attributed with having written "the first modern novel," "the first bilingual novel," and "the first scientific novel." If the strength of any of these categorizations and the extremism with which attempts are made to define Saizarbitoria's novels are disputable, it is true that the author's unrepentant seeking in each novel is significant in all its forms: thematic, technical, and linguistic.

The term "bilingual," as applied to his novel 100 metro, is rather ambiguous. The distribution of Spanish and Basque among the different voices heard in the novel is something more than a mimicking of reality. It is an implicit manifestation of the linguistic choice that every Basque author, given the strongly diglossic situation of the Basque language, is forced to make. With respect to the "scientific" language of his third novel, Ene Jesus, the label refers to his narrative style that springs from everyday living filtered through the author's intuition and narrative consciousness. Saizarbitoria often alludes to the urgent and complex problems of linguistic expression which confront the writer who decides to use the Basque language as a tool. His narrative is palpable proof of those difficulties. Each new novel is a different and rigorous attempt to tackle this unresolved, and perhaps unresolvable, problem.

Following Txillardegi and Saizarbitoria, other young writers have sprouted from the ever more leafy tree of Basque narrative. We still find authors from time to time, generally from the older generation, who cling to the anachronistic orthodoxy of the costumbrista novel or who, in any case, are strangers to the thematic and stylistic conventions of modern narratives. However, there is no doubt that the "old" Basque novel is no longer useful, either as a vision of the world or as literature, for describing the different and complex reality of the country nor for expressing the writer's new experience of reality and his or her personal understanding of the adventure of storytelling. This double challenge of reality and written expression is such that the Basque narrator cannot look back, for the past offers a meager literary tradition containing little of value for the new historical, cultural, and literary circumstance.

I mentioned above that the modernization of Basque narrative has been necessarily stated in terms of rupture, specifically with the costumbrista novel and its epistemological, ideological, and literary pretexts. But any rupture, no matter how historically legitimate, implies the traumatic and nearly fatal cutting of the umbilical cord linking the present to the past, and those things worth preserving are often carried away by the tide of the inevitable hemorrhage.

When we attend to the difficulties faced by today's narrative writers in solving the language and stylistic problems of their storytelling task, we would think that one of our costumbrista novelists such as Txomin Agirre, and perhaps even Etxeita, Anabitarte, or Erkiaga, would still have something to contribute to the formation of Basque narrative prose. The evolution of Agirre from his first novel, *Auñemendiko lorea*, to *Garoa* is readily apparent. Expressivity and flexibility of description, the mastery and agility of dialogue, the incorporation of colloquial expressions, etc., are accomplishments offered by more than one example of costumbrista prose that modern writers have not been able to appreciate and utilize. It is a great shame that those who are familiar with the old school, Agustin Zubikarai and Txomin Garmendia to name two, have insisted on writing novels that have already been written and which were anachronistic, both as a genre and an interpretation of reality, when they were written the first time.

The Search for Models

The "new" Basque novel—the narrative in general—thus was forced to look elsewhere for role models with which to confront the challenge that reality and literature posed for the writer. One might think that the shortest, most logical path would be recourse to Spanish narrative, it being the closest both geographically and linguistically, if we consider that the vast majority of the writers involved in the modernization of Basque narrative are also Spanish speakers. The exception is Jon Mirande, a Zuberoan born in Paris who learned Basque when he was twenty years old. His only novel, *Haur besoetakoa* (The Godchild), dates from 1970 and echoes the occasionally decadent but refined intellectual aestheticism of Gide or Montherlant.

However, Spanish writers are not the models which inspire the new Basque novelists, at least not in a visible and decisive way. This is surely due to the fact that the Spanish novel has not been a stylistic trendsetter in the evolution of contemporary narrative for the past forty years. Moreover, it is evident that Basque literature has strived, in poetry prior to the novel, to be in tune with the aesthetic pretexts and literary conventions of the cultural scene through thematic preoccupations and forms of expression. Most of today's Basque writers —poets and authors of prose alike—are quite familiar with the literatures of Europe and America. It is against them, against their more accepted and influential manifestations and expressions, that Basque writers measure the tone and rhythm of the modernization of Basque literature.

The influence of these other literatures can be readily observed. We alluded above to the existential root of the problems Txillardegi posed in his first novel, an existentialism that persisted in his 1960 work, *Peru Leartza'ko* (Peter of Leartza), united there with a keen interest in oriental philosophy and spirituality. In Saizarbitoria's book *Ene Jesus* there are clear echoes of the Irish novelist Samuel Beckett. This is due not to the name of the main character, Samuel, but to the work's elemental and larvalike universe, fetally enclosed on itself, within which action (if there is any) transpires, and because of a demanding and rigorous refinement of the narrative style.

The so-called boom in Latin American literature has had a clear, understandable, and continuing influence on the new Basque narrative. Angel Lertxundi, one of the most established and personal voices in today's Basque literature, was surely the first to introduce to the Basque novel narrative keys and styles of literary interpretation of reality that remind us of the persuasive and much-used "magic realism" of the Latin Americans. Lertxundi's sociomythological interpretation of Euskadi in his first novel, *Ajea du Urturik* (Something's Wrong with Urturi), 1971, reminds us of the universe created in a masterful and exemplary manner by García Márquez in his famous novel *A Hundred Years of Solitude*: a universe both real and symbolic, magical and yet historical. Lertxundi's novel *Hamaseigarrenean aidanez* (The Sixteenth Time's the Charm), 1983, also brings to mind the Colombian Nobel Prize winner. The exposition and narrative development of its plot, the life and tragic end of an inveterate bettor, is reminiscent of the storytelling technique used in García Márquez's *Crónica de una muerte anunciada* (Chronicle of a Death Foretold).

Falling within this same sphere of Latin American influence, we find the universe and narrative organization of the 1982 novel *Poliedroaren hostoak* (The Leaves of the Polyhedron) by Joan Mari Irigoien, one of the few long novels in Basque literature—ambitious and interesting as a literary offering, though not entirely successful. Nevertheless, a novel as "different" (for many reasons) as was *Poliedroaren hostoak* deserved more attention than it received from readers and critics.

Regardless of what I have said about the models which inspire the new Basque narrative, one should not believe that the Basque novel is limited to mere mechanical imitation of other literary interpretations of reality or imported narrative techniques, simply aping authors and works placed in the glare of the literary present by fashion or the critics. There is enough linguistic, thematic, and narrative originality in the Basque authors and works cited above to issue them a certificate of authenticity in modern Basque literature. Of course, there is a danger in following models, and Basque literature is not immune from it. At any rate, rather than looking for analogies and parallels between authors and their works and making superficial and meaningless comparisons, it is more interesting to point out the profuse and sometimes hurried incorporation of new techniques and modes of storytelling by Basque novelists that began with the revolution of the novel in the 1920s.

In contrast to the simple, monolithic, single-voiced view of reality of the costumbrista writers and their linear, problem-free, uniform way of expressing this reality, the new Basque narrative must look for techniques capable of expressing the problematic and complex nature of its own reality, the numerous visions of it that an author can present, and the ambiguity of any attempt to describe it literarily.

In other words, the question that arises when a Basque author begins a new narrative is not only which world view of Basque reality shall be portrayed in the novel but also how the language itself—its expressive and representative possibilities—shall be used. It is perhaps here, on the level of language and narrative techniques, that the turning point of the modern Basque narrative is most blatantly obvious.

The self-sufficient and paternalistic omniscient narrator of the costumbrista novel has given way to narrators who adopt more diverse and sometimes more elaborate styles of narration by use of grammatical persons which are totally new to Basque literature. The same thing occurs with time. The Balzac-like treatment of time in the costumbrista novel as an exterior and chronological phenomenon has given way to an interior Proustian concept of time, an inner time belonging to the consciousness around which the novel's universe is built and which ultimately determines the style of narration.

The multiplicity of planes of action and temporal axes, the ever-more frequent use of anachronism, the predominance of introspection, and the utilization of retrospective techniques are some of the more notable consequences of this new way of seeing and resolving the problems that time poses for the writer, both in fiction and in discourse.

The result is the variety and richness of the new Basque novel as opposed to the plain, monotonous uniformity of the costumbrista narration. Consequently, today's narrative is better adapted to a social and cultural reality characterized by complexity, mobility, and contrasts: a reality which, in the final analysis, runs circles around the static Manichaean duality of the romantic costumbrista genre.

Development of Modern Basque Narrative

While the break with the costumbrista novel started in 1957 with the publication of *Leturiaren egunkari ezkutua*, that does not mean that the panorama of Basque narrative has changed substantially since that date. Txillardegi's novel was the only one published in Basque that year. The two that appeared in 1958, *Poli* by Agustín Anabitarte and *Arranegi* by Eusebio Erkiaga, did not follow, either thematically or stylistically, the new path initiated by Txillardegi. Rather, they were written in an orthodox style in the purist tradition of the Basque costumbrista genre. Anabitarte had already written two books of this type in 1931 and 1932. As for Erkiaga, he offers little, either in *Arranegi* or in his subsequent novels, that appears to be even minimally innovative beyond his modest attempt to use the city—the urban milieu—as his setting. In this period, specifically between 1957 and 1968, four or five other novels appeared which offer no positive contribution to the development of Basque letters, and whose authors have not published any other titles.

There was a turnaround in 1964, after nearly ten years of silence, by the great narrative writer Yon Etxaide with his novel *Gorrotoa lege* (The Law of Hate). Almost four hundred pages long, it is an absolutely exceptional phenomenon in Basque narrative, in which he maintains the historical and legendary themes of his previous novels.

In 1967, there appeared the book *Gauaz ibiltzen dana* (The Night Walker), considered relatively important from more than one perspective. First, the author, Txomin Peillen, the one French-Basque who has entered the world of the twentieth-century novel, did so through the genre of the detective story, a genre with little precedent in Basque literature. José Antonio Loidi successfully launched the Basque detective novel in 1956 with *Amabost egun Urgain'en* (Two Weeks in Urgain). In 1962, Mariano Izeta's *Dirua galgarri* (Money is Perdition) again treats the detective theme that Peillen will later cultivate.

An especially significant date in the development of the modern Basque novel is surely 1969: First of all, because of the number of novels (four) published that year, including Txillardegi's third novel, *Elsa Scheelen*. Secondly, two new names were added to the body of Basque narrative writers who were to attain, though for different reasons and from different perspectives, an important place in the history of the contemporary Basque novel. They were Ramón Saizarbitoria and Xabier Gereño.

We have seen above that Saizarbitoria played a primordial role in modernizing Basque narrative, not only with his first novel, *Egunero hasten delako*, but also with his second and third. Gereño's importance, on the other hand, is a different matter. To begin with, he is the most prolific writer of contemporary Basque literature. He has tried his hand at the most diverse of genres: the social novel, the detective novel, the historical novel, humor, etc., as well as various forms of the popular novel. Gereño's enthusiasm and indefatigable dedication to literature are, to be sure, laudable. However, a greater effort in the area of execution and technique, as well as greater literary autonomy, would have been desirable.

Beginning in the 1970s, Basque narrative appears to be more and more conscious of its identity as a literary genre, of new themes offered for consideration, and of new technical and stylistic possibilities placed at its disposal by the development of contemporary narrative. The narrative genres, specifically the novel, have solidified their status within literature. This institutionalization of narrative prose within Basque literature and culture was first represented in quantitative terms, since, from 1969 on, the number of narrative writers and Basque-language narrative works increases progressively.

Limiting ourselves to the novel, a few statistics should be sufficient. In the first stage of Basque narrative prose, characterized by the dominance of the costumbrista novel and spanning the fifty-eight years between 1898 and 1956, nineteen novels were published in Basque. In the thirty short years since the dawning of the new Basque novel in 1957, about a hundred have been published, 85 percent since 1969. On the other hand, all the novelists who published after this date, with the exception of Txillardegi and Peillen, are newcomers to Basque literature.

Narrative writers like Saizarbitoria, Lertxundi, Arantxa Urretavizcaya, Koldo Izagirre, José Agustín Arrieta, and, among the younger ones, Bernardo Atxaga and Joseba Sarrionaindia, represent modernity, exacting literary standards, and an aesthetic quality that Basque narrative prose previously lacked. In more than one instance there are texts that compare favorably with representative examples of narrative from other languages.

However, the merit or significance of modern Basque narrative should not be measured by a comparison of qualities—an elusive and difficult task in the case of literatures in different languages—but rather by the conscientious, laborious, and positive efforts by Basque writers to place their work in the same thematic and stylistic orbit as the great contemporary novels. In this way, we can explain the Basque novel's openness to a great variety of genres, techniques, styles, and fictional worlds, an openness that has resulted in an enrichment and modernization of the narrative and Basque literature as a whole, and its institutionalization within Basque culture. In my opinion, it is literary prose, fiction in particular, that created the basis for the new status of written literature in Basque culture.

Lyricism in Basque writing is directly linked to the popular tradition of oral poetry, a natural development as a society becomes conscious of its linguistic and cultural identity and tries to express it in written form. Narrative literature, without roots in the oral tradition (although there is an important narrative ingredient in some forms of popular poetry), presupposes a new consciousness of literature as a linguistic and cultural practice. This consciousness is expressed not only from the point of view of the writer, or more properly the creation, but also has consequences for other mediums that channel the social function of written literature, such as the book of literary prose (the "irakurgayak," which were the first novels) and the individual act of reading. The novel, or in more general terms, narrative prose, has substantially altered the sociocultural status of Basque literature, and opened up not only the possibility of a new literary genre in all its different forms, but also a new mode of identification in the face of reality and writing.

Basque poetry has had a longer life and higher aesthetic values than has the narrative, but it is through narrative that written Basque literature has embarked on the road to maturity and crossed the threshold into the modern world. This is the context in which we should place the quantitative and qualitative development of modern Basque narrative in order to measure the transcendence of its function and meaning in Basque literary history. The increase of writers who, since 1969, have cultivated narrative forms, particularly the novel, has produced an interest in more varied types of works in line with what is taking place in the contemporary Western novel and in contrast with the absolute predominance of the costumbrista school in previous times.

The current nature of the detective novel, pioneered by writers such as Peillen, Gereño, and Gotzon Garate, is worthy of mention and should be explained not so much as a continuation of the trail blazed by Loidi in 1956, but rather as analogous with that which has ultimately occurred in other narratives. Along with its strength as one of the most typical and successful forms of the popular novel, the detective story has been elevated aesthetically and thematically through the literary treatment that certain authors have given it.

Equally worthy of mention is the renewed interest in historical themes, also in line with what has been happening in the literatures of other languages. But it should not be forgotten that the Basque novel began at the end of the nineteenth century as historical fiction and that Etxaide, on three occasions, has also attempted historical-legendary themes. However, the recent recourse to history by Mario Onaindia in his 1984 novel *Gilen Garateako batxilera* (Gilen of Garate, Graduate) supposes a concept of the historical novel that is ideologically and technically different from that found in Agirre or Etxaide, and even different from Gereño's historical works. Curiously, however, the contemporary Basque novel has barely touched upon either distant or recent Basque history, and although it might evoke poetic documentation of collective memory, it can only do so with difficulty.

With their lively curiosity about every aspect of the contemporary novel, Basque writers could not fail to attempt purely experimental or automatic writing, and that is what Patri Urkizu tried with the unending interior monologue of his 1975 work *Sekulorum sekulotan* (Through Centuries of Centuries). Historically speaking, perhaps it was necessary, if not inevitable, for fictional prose to explore the infinite tunnel of experimentation, but it has done so with neither the interest nor the literary quality of Harzábal's experimental lyric poetry.

Finally, it should be pointed out that Basque narrative writers have been showing a growing interest in situating their fictional worlds within their characters, reaching exterior reality by means of the narrative filter of consciousness. It might be too pretentious to speak of a psychological novel, but the novelists are scrutinizing the intricate labyrinths of their characters' consciousnesses more closely, and the protagonist's psychological reality decides not only the organization and development of the theme, but also its narrative treatment. If we have already looked down the murky well of dissatisfied consciousness through the confessional writing in the secret diary of Leturia, the psychological digging goes even deeper in a novel like *Haur besoetakoa*, in spite of the usage of a less confidential and more objective narrative perspective. In any case, the primacy of the consciousness is the result of an undeniable orientation in the new Basque novel (and to some extent, in the short story) towards lyricism, a movement already begun by Txillardegi.

Lyricism in the Modern Basque Novel

Without a doubt, lyricism is one of the clearest and most widespread characteristics of modern Basque narrative prose, and it coincides with a direction often taken by the novel in other contemporary literatures. If the concept of the lyrical novel, already recognized by literary theory and modern criticism, does not offer clearly defined profiles, it is evident that the revolution in fiction, beginning at the turn of the century, has swept across conventional frontiers of the genre, and a form of epic lyricism in the guise of the novel has been systematically incorporating thematic, expressive, and technical elements of the lyric approach. This refinement of the ego, as the focus of the vision and the means necessary to achieve reality, results in a mode of fictional representation that is more and more aptly named the lyric novel. The Basque narrative has been heading more firmly in this direction since the beginnings of its modernization.

The lyrical dimension of Txillardegi's *Leturiaren egunkari ezkutua* lies not only in the self-confessional nature of the story, but also in the romantic-existential consciousness that filters, colors, and determines the interpretation of objective reality. This process of lyrical refinement of exterior reality is taken to its very limits by Txillardegi himself in his 1979 novel *Haizeaz bestaldetik* (Beyond the Wind) to the point that the text barely subscribes to the genre's essential conventions. This work is a lyrical narrative poem in prose, a mythical and poetic autobiography, a more lyrical than epic attempt at a symbolic-existential reinterpretation of the ego in the world. Critics consciously avoid classifying *Haizeaz bestaldetik* as a novel, even a lyrical novel, because it does not lend itself very easily to either classification.

At any rate, every time Txillardegi has returned to the novel it has been not so much to tell a story as to state something about himself. The path leading from *Leturiaren egunkari ezkutua* to *Haizeaz bestaldetik* is a path of adventure, crisis, and personal utopia. The name of the protagonist, whether Leturia, Peru de Leartza, or the anonymous Ego living in an agonizing incertitude between the Sea and the Lake, is not important.

This sort of lyrical seclusion in the inner worlds of the consciousness, mediating an exit through introspection and memory toward exterior realities, is common among today's Basque narrative writers, though not as radically as in Txillardegi. The following examples of this lyrical seclusion are not an exhaustive list by any means.

The universes in Saizarbitoria's novels also appear to be filtered through subjectivity. In this respect, the way in which the author treats the plot of his second novel, 100 metro, is quite significant. The book is about the last one hundred meters of the escape of a Basque activist in a square in Donostia (San Sebastián) before he is shot down by pursuing policemen. The fugitive reminisces as he runs, and the plot of the novel is divided into the consciousness of the character at different times and during different actions. Moreover, the escape itself is narrated in a rhetorical and autoreflexive second person that turns the objective fact of escape into subjective consciousness and feeling. The importance of the internalization of the action, and how it is filtered through the narrating and reminiscing consciousness of the character, has not been sufficiently studied for the theme of the novel 100 metro, nor is this the moment to do so.

The internalization of action and the retrospective medium of the consciousness also provided the thematic and narrative framework for Haranburu Altuna's simple and well-written 1973 novel Itsasoak ez du esperantzarik (The Sea Is Without Hope), and for Arantxa Urretavizcaya's excellent and charming short novel Zergatik panpox (Why, Darling?), published in 1979. In that work, Basque prose reached a level of lyrical refinement that has not been achieved since by any other writer. For instance, the woman chosen by Mario Onaindia as the letter-writing narrator in his 1983 novel Grand Placen aurkituko gara (We'll Meet at Grand Square) seems to have neither the authenticity nor the strength and delicacy of the protagonist in Zergatik panpox.

The feminine soul, feminine consciousness, and love relationships from a woman's perspective have found a unique representation through Urretavizcaya: a representation that is more authentic, more vigorous, and more tender than that of any other Basque narrative writer. It would be an oversimplification to attribute this to the author's femaleness. The ultimate and fundamental reason for her success is that she is, above all else, a great writer.

José Agustín Arrieta also filters his story through consciousness and memory in his 1979 novel *Abuztuaren 15eko bazkalondoa* (After Lunch on August 15th). This is done by means of family scenes during a hot and festive summer afternoon. The protagonist's biography is revealed as a collective family and social chronicle through a loving and keen remembrance of his father, and the whole of the story is narrated in a reminiscing first person that organizes, judges, emphasizes, and tells the story.

In Angel Lertxundi's novel, *Hamaseigarrenean aidanez*, the central motive of the plot, the adventures of the die-hard gambler Domingo who ultimately meets a silly and tragic end, is counterbalanced by the inner feelings of his wife Marcelina, a mute spectator to the tragedy, and by the highly subjective mode of telling the story to the rhythm of an inquest carried out by the narrator.

I believe that these examples are more than enough to demonstrate the glide of modern Basque narrative toward a way of viewing and representing reality that is more lyrical than epic. There is a marked preference for interior universes or, in any case, for filtering the experience of reality through the consciousness of a first-person narrator. One might say there is a kind of fear of the outside, of describing it with naked objectivity, as if the writer has nothing to say about anything beyond his own experience.

Naturally, from the subjectivity of the ego, upon which both the discourse and the story are built in the first place, in many cases there is an opening to wider universes which are no longer individual, but rather social and political. This is so, for instance, in *100 metro*, *Abuztuaren 15eko*, and *Hamaseigarrenean aidanez*, but the authors never manage to cut the cord that links the story to the consciousness that lives it, remembers it, and recounts it. Indeed, any story told emerges at the precise point where the writer encounters exterior reality. From this juncture on, the writer can drift toward an outer objectivity or crawl back into the inner space of the ego and the consciousness. The latter is preferred by modern Basque writers.

Due to its intimate nature, the Basque novel is in no way a chronicle of reality and collective experience, but neither was the costumbrista novel (because of its idealism). It seems as if Basque writers are afraid to face historical and social reality, be it past or present, or fear telling a story from the detached viewpoint of an external and objective narrator. Indeed, they hardly dare to tell a story at all, beyond a more or less disguised personal experience, and there is a strong tendency to set the narrative focus in the character's own consciousness as well as an almost instinctive resistance to breaking the expressive shackles that lyrically bind the author to reality and the written word. Could this be due to an ancestral attraction to lyricism, so firmly rooted in the Basque literary tradition? Or is it simply a manifestation in Basque literature of a feature common in contemporary narrative—the progressive dissolution of the line between the epic and the lyrical?

The history of Basque literature itself, with a tradition of written poetry dating from the sixteenth century, as opposed to a narrative that did not establish itself until well into the twentieth, would add a special emphasis to the lyrical as opposed to the real, even when it is a matter of expressing objective worlds independent of the activity of the narrator's consciousness.

The attitude of the epic in the face of reality, which modern bourgeois society expresses literarily through the novel, was fully identified and established in the great realistic novels of the nineteenth century. Novelists like Balzac, Dickens, Galdos, and later Thomas Mann and our own Baroja are exceptional witnesses and chroniclers of a time in history that lives in their writings, poeticized and mythicized without ceasing to be a part of social reality.

The Basque novel has not gone through the experience of fictionalized realism, since it has necessarily had to go from prerealism (or strongly regionalist literature which some of today's scholars define as essentially "antinovel") to the most modern and avant-garde forms. In thirty short years the Basque narrative has had to traverse a path that was so complicated that it could not avoid being affected by the process. Perhaps it is like a child who grows prematurely and, having grown tall before his time, still cannot hide certain physical inadequacies. The Basque narrative is experiencing a growth crisis, which is the basis for explaining its many virtues and undeniable limitations.

The Future of the Basque Narrative

Perhaps the vision of the contemporary Basque narrative on these pages seems pretentious and overly optimistic. Nevertheless, I believe

I have been objective insofar as objectivity is possible in areas such as criticism or literary history, where every interpretation wears a veneer of subjectivity, minimal though it may be. However, it is not a question of reaching for unreasonable objectivity. In any case, if an insufficiently proven statement has been made, something no work of literary criticism can avoid, I hope the reader will accept it as a hypothesis subject to revision and verification by much-needed subsequent research on modern Basque narrative.

It is fair to state that the outlook for the Basque narrative is positive and promising, especially when we take into account the history of Basque literature and its current state. The narrative genre, in the form of novel, novella, short story, etc., overtook poetry, even in terms of statistics according to figures for Basque-language publications in 1984. This occurred in spite of the fact that poetry is the most established and literarily mature genre, a genre in which Basque literature has reached its most important levels.

Nevertheless, the increase of narrative prose at the expense of poetry is yet more revealing proof of the depth of the socioliterary establishment of a new genre in Basque tradition, one that occupies the same niche that written narratives occupy in more developed literary systems with even longer traditions. It is in the narrative, because of the precariousness of its origins, where we may best measure the laborious efforts of contemporary writers to place Basque literature in the same orbit as that occupied today by the great Western literatures.

This optimistic analysis of Basque narrative is, nevertheless, still ambivalent. On one side of the coin are its achievements and on the other some undeniable limitations and grave problems which must be specified and confronted by writers and the literary establishment in general. In closing, I would like to point out some of these problems.

In modern Basque narrative, the novel is more cultivated than the short story. I omit children's literature, for although it is a growing field, it does not normally determine trends and development in the evolution of literature. In reality, we should be talking about the short novel, since most Basque novels are under two hundred pages and only two or three surpass three hundred pages. To be sure, the length of the book is not a rigorous criterion for the classification of narrative forms within a genre, but it can at least serve as an indicator of a real limitation on the universes which the Basque novelist confronts, and of the low intensity of the enthusiasm for the epic that inspires and motivates the way the novel reflects reality. In Basque there are short novels full of brilliant passages, but there are those that lack completeness and seem to be outlines of long novels with respect to length of narration, amplitude, and intensity of epic vision, which the writers did not know how, or did not dare, to implement. This, in my opinion, is what happened with Saizarbitoria's 100 metro.

On the other hand, the indiscriminate cultivation of different literary genres is commonplace among modern Basque writers. A good many of the writers cited here are also poets, and indeed the writer who cultivates the novel or short story exclusively is the exception. Angel Lertxundi and Mikel Zarate are two who have dedicated themselves exclusively to the novel and short story, and who have done so with an awareness of the nature and poetic-stylistic demands of each narrative form.

Sometimes one has the impression that the short story is seen as a lesser genre—not only as far as length is concerned but also in terms of quality—a pastime for the long, silent moments inherent in the maturing of a novel, or a testing ground until the writer sets out to tackle the greater and more important genre. In fact, there are no narrative writers who can be definitively identified as short-story writers. The young writers who have debuted in the world of Basque literature with a short story, such as Mikel Hernández Abaitua, Joseba Sarrionaindia, and Laura Mintegi, are all expected to go on to write novels. They *should* go on to novels and they will. (Curiously, as I am writing these lines I have learned that Laura Mintegi has won the Azkue Prize for Literature with her novel Bai baina . . . ez [Yes But Not Quite].)

José Irazu, writing as Bernardo Atxaga, deserves special mention as he is without a doubt the most personal, vigorous, and promising voice in Basque literature today. With works such as his 1976 novel Ziutateaz (About the City) and his 1978 work Etiopia (Ethiopia), and as a pioneer of a kind of Basque literary "underground" movement with journals such as Panpina ustela (Rotten Doll) and Pott (Tuckered Out), he has brought an undeniable modern dimension to the novel, if not a complete break with the past. In his books, Atxaga blurs the conventional boundaries between the literary genres. Every new title means another brilliant step along the rigorous path of linguistic and literary discovery that he has been following. And finally, he has caught our attention and provided the catalyst for projects in recent literature, the role and significance of which cannot yet be surmised.

The first problem confronting today's Basque writer, and for that matter Basque literature in general, is the language itself. The great majority of current Basque writers were debuted through Unified Basque or "Euskara Batua," the language proposed by the Academy of the Basque Language, Euskaltzaindia. But linguists do not make a language, speakers do, and it is evident that this abstract model, this system of spelling conventions and phonetic and morpho-syntactic rules, needs an expressive and stylistic fleshing out that only writers can provide.

With the coldness of a "prefabricated" model on one hand and a fragmenting dialectal dispersion on the other, the continual creation of language, which is the primary vocation of every poet, doubly challenges the Basque writer because the very system of linguistic-literary registers must be wrought day after day by hammering out the written word itself and not, as is the case in other languages, by merely employing different stylistic usages within the register.

These language problems are particularly evident in narrative prose and are much more pressing than in poetry. The language of narration is polyphonic and poses the problem of linguistically and stylistically expressing the different voices heard in every narrative discourse.

Along with this quest for linguistic expression are other needs, no less essential, that also affect the Basque-language writer of narrative prose. In the first place, once the shackles that tied Basque prose to the costumbrista tradition were broken, it was necessary to look for new technical and stylistic forms to express experience through literature. In this laborious and unavoidable quest for form, one sometimes gets the impression that the authors can't see the forest for the trees in that today's Basque writers occasionally get lost in the intricate labyrinths of ultramodern techniques that I myself have termed "an inflation of form." In their desire to adapt Basque narrative language to that of more developed literatures, Basque writers sometimes give the impression that they know how to say it but have nothing to say.

Despite the fact that narrative is established as a genre within the Basque literary system, it still has not taken on a solid identity. It is ingenuous to think that Basque narrative could be identified by traits other than the language itself, although this has been possible in other contemporary literatures, of which the Latin American novel is only one example.

At this point I would suggest that the essential task for the Basque novel is the blending of the techniques and styles of narrative with the individual, social, and collective experience and mythology that the novel is witness to, for this is its original purpose: man, while he exists and in order to live, will, like Scheherazade, always need to tell stories and have stories told. In the end, one has the impression that our narrative writers have not yet told us what we were, what we are, or what we would like to be. The Stendahl-like mirror of the Basque novel has barely begun to reflect the path of our dreams and experiences.

JOSÉ LUIS
ALVAREZ EMPARANZA
(TXILLARDEGI)

(b. 1929)

A linguist and industrial engineer, José Luis Alvarez Emparanza, known as Txillardegi, arrived on the Basque narrative scene at a time when stylistic and thematic modernization were just beginning. He belongs to the generation that, in the sixties, began to write from unorthodox perspectives both ideologically and aesthetically, in keeping with the new philosophies of existentialism and Marxism that thrived in Europe.

The protagonist of his first novel Leturiaren egunkari ezkutua, published in 1957, was the first problematic hero of Basque literature, and the style of the work suggests a narrative and thematic break with the romantic tradition of the costumbristas that had existed in the Basque novel since its birth in the late nineteenth century.

Existential reflection is present to some degree in all of his novels. It appears in Peru Leartza'ko (1960) and Elsa Scheelen (1968). In Haizeaz bestaldetik (Beyond the Wind), published in 1979, this existential reflection is extended to autobiography. The following text is a chapter from that novel. The lyrical nature of the book is emphasized by frequent use of free verse. The work has an apocalyptic tone, and the power of Txillardegi's language and abundant vocabulary is evident.

Beyond the Wind

CHAPTER FIVE

And it might have been the following day at sundown, when the day was steeped in a strange salty odor, that I approached Guéthary alone. From above the town, the distant roar of the ocean could be heard.

> . . . and you calmed
> my thirst for stillness
> at least for a moment;
> even if you lit within me forever
> the most unceasing anxiety,
> and injected me with the most painful
> pain of the Sea.

There was no one on the main street that runs down from the post office. In the quiet, two silent threads of trees. A single-walled handball court, empty. The hotels were also empty. Most of the stores, closed. Only a couple of women, chatting untiringly by the candy store on the left.

And as I approached the beach, the roar of the Sea grew louder.

I crossed the bridge over the train tracks and left behind the Mimiague bookstore and the Gurutzia hotel.

As if we were drowning, like crazy people, we embraced; and in that endless stream of kisses, we fell upon the bed. . . . Do you remember?

And we both heard promises and sighs that are not usually heard; and we saw and touched soft garments that are not usually seen or touched. And we reached heights of pleasure and joy that are impossible to reach twice in one lifetime . . .

. . . And like a thousand other times, I went to the small lookout platform adorned with tamarind trees.

And things I had said and heard came to my mind time and again, things I had left far behind, an obsessive theme; and I thought I saw you above the waters of the Sea, as if that growing fog formed itself in your image.

And I called to you:

> ... come quickly, I pray you,
> at least once,
> I want to hear
> your laughter
> and your voice
> at least
> one more time!

> ... once again
> I want to hide
> your cold hands
> in mine,
> as I did yesterday
> in the warm
> languid morning!

But my pleas were useless!

And upon speaking the word "yesterday," it was as if I woke up.

"When was this yesterday? . . . After all, the clocks haven't stopped."

And saddened by the very enormity of your happiness, you said to me:

"Never forget these hours! . . . Please, never forget me! . . . No matter what happens, I'll never love anyone but you! . . . I couldn't . . . Even after you die, after everyone has forgotten you, long after, as long as I'm alive, you will live within me . . . If the bitterness of life ever drives you to despair, remember my undying words!"

And in that way, for the first and last time, you and I together learned what it is to spend an entire night without sleeping, just talking, and smiling, and laughing.

It was as if the entire night only lasted a few minutes. . . .

But on the thunderous evening that followed, you didn't appear at the lookout point in Guéthary. You will never come to me again!

I didn't know it then. Not then, but now, on this second voyage from beyond the wind, I know . . . that warm, languid morning is gone forever.

. . . And from the lookout, I saw how the waves crashed against the rocks on the right, and how crests of foam rose above them; and how they changed a few meters further on into foamless waves again.

And I observed those fleeting crests moving in rows as if fleeing from each other; waves erasing each other, one after another, before they reached the beach, until they were gone, leaving behind an area covered with foam.

And I was frightened.

"Destined to disappear, one after the other, without reaching the beach!"

And like the Basque poet who saw the immaculate snowflake disappear the instant he held it in his hand, I found myself with all my dreams turned to foam at the moment I possessed them.

I saw the rocks thrusting out of the water, the waves crashing endlessly against them. And truly, at low tide, the Sea felt farther away to me; much farther away and more foreign than the day before seemed, although it seemed far away also. And the secluded beaches of Bidart seemed wider and emptier to me than that warm, languid morning.

And it seemed the emptiness and the salt air had compressed themselves into the seacoast below Guéthary.

That for which I had waited for so long, that which I had deeply desired and greatly loved, at the very moment it came to me . . . seemed like a distant memory, and turned into bitter despair.

And over the roar of the waves, the words of the singer from the North ring in my memory:

> rocks
> that the tides wash over
> whose hearts are forever
> at low ebb . . .

And unable to assimilate so much sadness, I looked behind me:
"It's impossible!"

But yes, the Gurutzia hotel was really closed, and the humble Mimiague bookstore was also closed; and all the other hotels and houses were closed as well. It wasn't just a bad dream.

And then I looked to my left and I saw that the Guéthary boardinghouse was vacant and run-down, all its green windows shuttered.

As it happens in incomprehensible dreams, I was the only living soul in Guéthary.

On that mild fall day, the sky was gray and the approach of winter was palpable.

And leaving the small lookout platform, I skirted the wall in front of it and headed down the path lined with tamarind trees.

Night was falling.

And I headed for Bidart on the little road at the top of the beach; and a little farther on, I jumped onto the sand. And driven by a strange internal force, I wrote these words on a patch of sand recently washed by the Sea:

When you arrive at the summit, the abyss is near.

And continuing northward on the smooth part of the beach, I walked, lost in thought, at the edge of the Sea, occasionally splashed by the foam of the waves:

"Why did you never return to me?"

And I felt sharp pain in my chest and an aching emptiness.

And I saw that the unequaled and unrepeatable happiness of that former day was quickly fading from me; and the process of this annihilation was well advanced after a period of seven times seven weeks:

> . . . yesterday morning,
> perhaps a morning of a year ago,
> or even better, an ancestral morning,
> that is already a distant morning of the past . . .
> and the languor of that distant morning
> and the warmth of that languorous morning,
> and the penetrating smell of saltwater . . .

. . . do you remember? . . . it's fading away . . . it's gone!

> . . . and I, a poor man,
> who once thought
> that the intensity of that warm, languorous morning
> would last forever,
> here I am today
> in this immediate day after,
> immersed in a hopeless hopelessness . . .

. . . fading away . . . erased . . . wiped out! For "time comes and robs you of love" . . .

On the other hand, there was the Sea, forgetful but unforgettable! The Sea was the only victor. A solid witness to human destiny, a lasting witness, a vile and merciless witness.

The Sea: too wide, too peaceful, too immense.

And I remembered the message from beyond the wind:

"The Sea is suitable only for the Sea. Your place is the lake."

And I began to understand my mistake:

> Why did you make me taste
> the fever of love,
> that maddening fever?
> Why did you have me cherish
> so briefly,
> so superbly,
> "that fleeting glimpse of the Infinite"?
> if later, for a long time,
> for a very long time,
> yea, for an eternity,
> I shall continue to suffer
> until my dying day,
> suffer infinite
> longing?

> Why did you make me
> smell the subtle aroma of the Sea?
> could it be that you did not know
> that this burning desire for happiness
> would transform us
> into the origin of all misfortune,
> the key to all tortures?

I assumed then there was a pine forest in the rain: "If only I hadn't slid down to the Tubuai!"

> "I love,
> love
> our countryside
> when the fog
> hides it from me . . ."

And I discovered that those moments of happiness were more fleeting than I thought, and that they were lost forever.

And it seemed that, until then, I had never truly understood what the Sea is and what it means.

And while night was falling, I wanted to enjoy the bygone scent of the saltwater, the nostalgic, far-away aroma of the Sea, so I headed up among the low tamarind trees and sat down on the grass in the center of a hill and looked at the Sea.

And I thought I saw you again, once and a thousand times; as if you yourself were the Sea.

And to the left and right I found that the fierce sea winds of Guéthary had twisted the tamarinds and the shrubs until they were partially uprooted; and their desire to live had hurt them and made them ugly; their desperate need to cling to the earth had deformed them and stripped them of their leaves; as if they had been wounded and stretched a thousand times in a never-ending battle.

How cruel the sea wind is!

How cruel, especially in summer!

And the water retreats, farther and farther.

And the sharp needles of rock rise up from the surface of the water at Koskene Point, as if begging the heavens, as if imploring: "Enough!"

But the Sea did not soften at all.

And I convinced myself that I must forget the Sea.

JOSÉ AGUSTÍN

ARRIETA

(b. 1949)

Arrieta debuted in Basque literature with a few short stories (Termitosti), and in 1978 he won the Ciudad de Irún prize for novels with Abuztuaren 15eko bazkalondoa (After Lunch on August 15th), an elaborately structured work with an autobiographical theme which is, at the same time, a chronicle of the history of San Sebastián during the 1950s and 1960s. By means of an after-dinner conversation, the past is described by those who fought and lost the war, and the present is described through the opinions and doubts of an adolescent seminarian.

Arrieta has also worked with written poetry (as opposed to the oral poetry of the Basque troubadours), as evidenced in his collections, Arrotzarena (The Foreigner's Poems) and Neurtitz neurgabeak (Unmeasured Verses), winner of the Ciudad de Irún prize for poetry in 1982. In his poetry we find carefully selected language and themes that continually allude to the characters, myths, and archetypes evoked in traditional Basque literature.

The following text is the penultimate chapter of the 1979 novel Abuztuaren 15eko bazkalondoa. In it we find the verbal unfolding of a dual personality, the protagonist and narrator, that seems to support the weight of a complex narrative organization rather well. Equally notable are Arrieta's descriptive details and his rich vocabulary, both characteristic of the novel.

After Lunch on August 15

CHAPTER NINE

You are alone in the kitchen when the doorbell rings. Six o'clock. The sound of hurried footsteps in the hall, a door opens and from the top of the stairs, "Who is it?," "Yes, I'm coming," a thrill of happiness in your sister's voice. Maybe they'll go to Mediola for a bite to eat, you think, they'll walk the little paths through the pine forest of Mount Ulia, they'll sit at the Whaler's Lookout for a long time staring out to sea, you imagine. Your sister tiptoes barefoot as silently as she can to the kitchen so as not to wake your sleeping parents. She's wearing a white short-sleeved dress. "And you? Don't you have to go out?" she asks you, putting on the slippers she keeps behind the kitchen cupboard. "No, a little later." "Okay, goodbye, little brother"; she comes close and offers you her cheek, your lips taste Nivea face cream in a fleeting sensation: your sister's tanned and shining face, arms, and legs, "goodbye, have fun," and Kit Carson's thick lips will explode against your sister's Nivea face and cocoa butter lips at the Whaler's Lookout on Mount Ulia, to the murmur of the waves—"and under the apple tree, under the eye of the moon—."

Maite's juggling apples on the stage in the square "—love has bloomed." There goes your sister spinning on her toes to the edge of the stage, there she goes now dragging her slippers softly across the carpet, and in the hall the loose plank creaks when she steps on it. Arantxa's coming, too, though no one has rung the doorbell for her. "Where are you going, Arantxa?"; she's going to Elizaran to the Sisters of Charity—she's been doing that a lot lately: is she thinking of becoming a nun?—she'll say the rosary with the sisters before the statue of the Virgin in the Milagrosa chapel, her friend Mari Asun will be there, too, and later they'll go up to the Elizaran terrace to eat pastry and drink a little sweet wine. She's wearing a long-sleeved blue dress, "See you later, squirt"—she still calls you that—, a kiss on the cheek, the off-white skin of her face, neck, and ankles. This summer she doesn't go to the beach at noon like me, you think, yes, she is surely planning to become a nun. There she goes down the hall, her black shoes rubbing softly against the carpet, goodbye "kantini" dancer. One, two, three jumps and you break the goblet, too bad, once again the plank in the hall creaks, unavoidably.

Well, I don't know. At Yosune's wedding, a couple of months ago, she stayed at the Rodil restaurant, even during the bebop. Perhaps her vocation is not very clear, because otherwise she would know that those of us whom Jesus has singled out must reject that kind of trashy ambience. And if I regret anything, it is precisely that. I didn't realize until Father Salvador told me, it never occurred to me that staying there did not suit me at all. What's more, as Father Fernando would say, "at the end of the day, you must show some deference to Christ," "deference." The decision should have come from myself, without waiting for Father Salvador. Forgive me, Jesus.

The music and shouting from the Rodil are far away when Father Salvador's car comes down Mount Ulia and turns into the Avenue of Navarra. The car's windshield wipers part the thin curtain of misty rain that's falling slowly and peacefully. As you put your raincoats on in the hall, the maître d' and two waiters say goodbye politely. "Yes, yes, the meal was excellent," Father Salvador tells them. Within five minutes I'll be in front of Sagrario, you think. The front seat of the red Seat 850, Father Salvador's black raincoat over his black cassock and sash. Yes, I had a nice time, Father Salvador, yes, I'm going to Saint Vincent's.

And now, too, it would be better for me, instead of staying here alone in the kitchen sweltering in this heat, to get up, wash my face, and go down to the dark coolness of the church, but you might say I find myself comfortable and at ease in this sultry heat that makes the atmosphere of the kitchen unbearable, while the seconds of six-I-don't-know-what-o'clock fall on the blue Formica tabletop like fat, sticky drops. The patio window is open and a gust of suffocating air from the clothesline upstairs attaches itself to your forehead, the fetid odor of a salted cod that Mrs. Bitxori has hung from a rusty nail by the window reaches your throat, and you notice once again how the warbling song of the partridge imprisoned in the cage on Mrs. Maria's cooler shimmers off the damp, cracked walls of the old patio. Other than that, silence reigns, silence and heat. The long after-lunch conversation is over. Better to close the patio window again, you decide, even though one never knows which is better, to have it open or closed.

I should take a nice swim, you think, belly up in the middle of the bay watching the lazy movements of the gulls. You take the glass in which you drank your Schweppes to the sink and go out of the kitchen into the dark hall. I really should take a nice swim, you think, your moccasin making the loose plank in the hallway squeak.

Even though the peace of absolution is spreading through your soul, even though the luminous twilight of this pretty corner of Saturrarán invites prayer and an appropriate atmosphere of spiritual peace, even though in a little while we are going to celebrate a truly moving paraliturgy in the little low-roofed chapel, Father, "I never stay at the beach any later than eleven." Pride, I must mention that in my next confession. *Mens sana in corpore sano.* "It's just that I don't find any other spiritual guide that I like in the parish." Perhaps I should tell you the whole truth in my next confession.

The peaceful waters of the bay under the cover of the gray morning clouds. You're all running on La Concha beach at nine-thirty in the morning. The blood pounds in your temples: inhaling through your nose, exhaling through your mouth, feet striking the hard, wet sand of the shoreline, Parrot's Beak hill, and start back. Soft, broken waves lap at your feet. To run well you must run on your toes, without your heels touching the ground, but you're tired already, you've begun to breathe through your mouth, you've started hitting the sand with your heels. I'll continue only up to that point, to the nightclub Eguzki. You have all reached it. Inhaling through the nose, exhaling through the mouth, inhale-exhale, crossing your arms, throwing them back, back, to strengthen your shoulder muscles, and expand your lungs. Now to the water, the three of you running, Jose Mari, Xanti, and you, running and jumping, tiny waves, the coolness of the water, let's do the crawl stroke as far as the barge. Breathe in next to the right shoulder, turning the neck a bit without lifting the head too much, because that slows you down; exhale forcefully under the water, blow and make bubbles but without opening the mouth too far, because then you swallow water; kick your feet continuously but not too high above the surface and without too much motion below the water because then you decrease, rather than increase, your speed.

And to keep from waking your parents from their nap, you tiptoe from the bathroom and head down the hall. When you go to open the front door, the loose board in the middle of the hallway creaks, and for a moment you are frozen at the door, neither advancing nor retreating, at the point where the weight of the sweltering kitchen air meets the promise of the cool breeze that filters through the shuttered dining room window. Muted by distance, the song of the partridge imprisoned on the patio reaches you there, and weakened by the thick window shutters, the sound of the people in the street and the music of a jota sung by a group of Navarrese friends leaving La Cepa tavern also reaches you there. Your face washed, your belly lightened of its overabundant lunch, your hair wet and parted on the side, there you are, wavering at the door to the street. A heavy sound penetrates the shutters. The bells of St. Vincent's clock resonate through the walls of the hallway. "Love one another as I have loved you." Sixteen years and suddenly you feel a nameless hatred there in the dark hallway. August 15, 1965. You hear your mother's cough, but soon it's silent again. You open the door and feel the fresh air at the head of the stairs, a freshness that increases as you descend. The first gust of wind from the street buffets you, "and the wheat is sprouting seeds," three men stand in front of the Cepa tavern, leaning on each other, the vibrant lament of a Navarrese jota explodes in the quiet street as it begins to fill with life, "that's why the farmers are singing." Couples pass by eating sea snails, young mothers push baby strollers, out to enjoy the fresh air, while you climb the gradual slope of San Telmo hill—how big it seemed to me when I was small, grandpa: "look out for the spirited horses," the lye maker's long wagon careens down the hill, perhaps its clanking brings a message from the sea. The sky is darkening and a north gale is coming. Sixteen years old and the heat of the day is almost over. As you reach the door of the Bathhouse, you take a deep breath of the fresh air. I could take a nice swim.

It's not very far to the floating platform. Your bodies bob on the calm sea, advancing rhythmically. Your arms splash noisily on the dark, meek surface of the sea. When the September tides come, you will not be able to leave the shore and immerse yourself in the bay, Father Michael will rent a rowboat and you'll go out there on the waves: hold on tight, huge waves are breaking! The invasion at Normandy: "fire one!" and one of you will pretend to be a torpedo and try to tip the boat, try to throw the others out, Father Michael is such a sportsman, he always wears a tee shirt over his bathing trunks. We've reached the floating platform. There are mollusks stuck to the flat bottom of the boat, black mollusks and black algae. Under its dark green skin the sea is a black morass. We have to dive off the diving board a few times. Jose Mari makes a frog dive, bravo, he went straight in, penetrating the soft surface with his arms perpendicular, Xanti made an "angel" dive, bravo, another perfect dive, now it's your turn. The board trembles beneath your feet, the sluggish mist is rising over the city hall and the Alderdi Eder park, the rays of the morning sun have shredded the fog, and a mastodon of a double-decker bus rolls by on Hernani Street, its windows twinkling, it's very easy: a tiny bounce, bend your body, hide your head between your arms, hands pointed like an arrow . . . , but after all that you still nearly belly flop again.

You've reached the railing along the Paseo Berria, the heat of this August 15 afternoon is giving way before the sea breeze, and you feel on your face a refreshing wind that heralds a northwester. The railing: sewage below, a gray spot spreads on the blue water around the ruins of a stone tower, sea gulls peck at the water and occasionally catch a small mullet. The sea gull's long, gray beak, and the mullet's silver-colored back, two fleeting shimmers reflecting the twilight. A nice swim, you think, a shower of clear water wetting you from head to toe, a sublime ablution that will clean you to the marrow, a gratifying baptism that will free you from the misery of all filth, *tota pulchra es Maria*. This place where the city's filth flows to the sea is where most of the mullet gather, but the gulls gather here, too. Here they all have a nice lunch, you think. And you imagine yourself in the middle of the bay, arms crossed, staring at the sky, bobbing on the waves. The hungry gulls dive again and again at the surface of the water. If you don't move, they'll think you're a dead fish. The white gulls will turn into black crows, the peaceful herring gulls into carrion-eating kestrels, you have to keep swimming, otherwise they will tear out your eyes, screeching and cawing. You can already feel the disgusting vultures tearing the flesh from your belly, your arms and legs feel paralyzed and you can't swim. But yes, I know how to swim and I go as far as the island almost every day with friends, you say to yourself, moving away from the railing and directing your gaze not at the filth on the water below but at the dark clouds that are starting to spread down the side of Mont Pas.

Thank goodness a storm is coming, thank goodness soon the clean foam of the waves will cover the filthy sewage—never, nowhere, no way, Lord, *fiat voluntas tua*, the feet of the Immaculate One crushed the serpent of sin forever—. Thank goodness the north wind has sprung from Mont Pas to chase away the heat.

You jump down from the pier and continue walking. The giant silhouette of the *Azor*[1] draws ever closer, there are motor launches and yachts anchored in its path. You have to rest before going on. A small yacht: *Iparra* is written in gold letters on its side. You grab hold of a lifesaver and prop your feet on the keel. How pleasant it is to be there, eyes closed, feeling your pulse pounding in your temples, letting the refreshing water eddy around your navel. But your feet, your feet are getting dirty on the smeared keel: sticky pieces of tar, difficult to remove even by scrubbing with a towel. You all decide to go up on deck. No one is aboard the ship at this hour, no one prevents you from going into the cabin and giving the ship's wheel a spin, but today the *Iparra*'s rudder is chained. You all lie down on the deck, on the wooden lattice, you close your eyes, and the light of the sun, peeking out from behind the clouds, leaks through your eyelids. You dream that, when you open your eyes, you will see a girl next to you, a girl with long hair and a smiling face, she'll offer you a drink in a soft voice, like they do in the secret-agent movies, she'll kneel down next to you and press her small firm breasts against your chest and lower her lips to yours, then you jump up: never, nowhere, no way, *tota pulchra es Maria*. The water of the bay is dark green, and the murmur of city traffic is far away.

Father Bernard the deacon, Father Bernard your exconfessor, found the comical anecdote you told about the incense on Easter Sunday at the main altar very funny. There he is, removing his vestments and folding them with great care on the tall, dark armoire in the sacristy, now he takes off his cingulum and smiles at you, and while your fellow seminarians tease you incessantly he takes the white alb off over his bowed head and smiles at you again. His black cassock is reflected in the big sacristy mirror, he approaches you in storklike strides and, ruffling your hair with one large hand, messing up the part you painstakingly combed before the mirror, he says, "Gone astray, gone astray."

It was not a scolding voice, you think now, leaving the railing and moving quickly along the Paseo Berria. I may just have time to walk the loop before it starts to rain. No, it wasn't a scolding voice. More likely he was thinking to himself, "Why don't you confess to me anymore?"

---

[1] Francisco Franco's yacht.

"I can't find another spiritual father in the parish that I like," you told Father Fernando in Harbide the truth, but not the whole truth. Still moving away from the railing, your pace quickens: when the tides of September and the implacable storms of winter arrive, the sea often breaks the railing, makes cracks in the asphalt, and floods your street.

BERNARDO ATXAGA

(b. 1951)

Atxaga appeared in Basque literature as an activist in the cultural underground through magazines like Panpina ustela (Rotten Doll) and Pott (Tuckered Out) as part of his decision to be a professional writer—not one who makes a living from writing but as one who lives for writing. With Atxaga literary activity achieves greater autonomy, a process that began in Basque literature in the sixties.

Atxaga has worked in various genres, such as children's stories and children's theater. His stories include "Nikolasaren abenturak eta kalenturak" (Adventures and Fevers of Nikolas) and "Ramuntxo detektibe" (Ramuntxo the Detective), both published in 1980. His plays, "Logalea zeuken trapezistaren kasoa" (The Case of the Sleepy Trapeze Artist) and "Zapatari ttikia" (The Little Shoemaker) were produced in 1981 and 1982 by a masked theater group. He has written the short novels Ziuta-teaz (About the City), published in 1976, and Bi anaia (Two Brothers), published in 1985. He received support from the Basque government while writing the latter. He received the Ciudad de Irún prize in 1982 for his story "Camilo Lizardiren erretorearen etxean aurkitutako gutunaren azalpena" (An Explanation of the Letter Found in the House of Parish Priest Camilo Lizardi), a work with stylistic overtones reminiscent of Juan Bautista Aguirre's Guipuzcoan classic of the history of Basque literature.

In his eagerness to try new forms of expression, he created a series of thirteen programs for Basque Television, "Idoia eta bere animaliak" (Idoia and Her Animals), composed of stories and rock 'n' roll songs also released as a phonograph recording.

The short story that follows is an example not only of Atxaga's mastery of the art of storytelling, but also of his continual questioning of the storytelling process, of writing, and of literature, which in large measure is the role Atxaga's work plays on the modern stage of Basque narrative.

A profound sense of irony, even satire, concerning reality and writing is another substantial characteristic of Atxaga's work as reflected in this short story.

To Write a Story in Five Minutes

In order to write a story in five minutes you need, in addition to the traditional pen and white paper, a miniature hourglass that tells you how much time has elapsed and at the same time demonstrates the futility of life and, consequently, your very activity while simultaneously denouncing it. Instead of staring at those monotonous monochrome walls, you should cast your gaze out the window at the wide panorama where gulls and other birds fly about in joyful geometry. Though not entirely necessary, it helps to listen to music. Once this is settled, turn your internal telescope inside yourself and ask if you're in a good mood, if you're hungry, or thirsty, or both, or have any other bodily concerns; if the answer is yes, for instance if you itch all over, do not despair, for it would be surprising if you were able to go straight to work on your first try. Note that, as yet, not half a minute has elapsed, get up and go in the kitchen, calm down, nothing unusual is happening. After drinking a glass of water and, even better, after splashing the nape of your neck with water, go to the bathroom before sitting down at the table again.

Over there are the sea gulls and over there are starlings, and right there, to the left of your bookcase, is a fat dictionary. Pick it up carefully, as if it were charged with electricity. Write the following sentence down on a page: "In order to write a story in five minutes, you need . . ." Now you have your beginning; barely two minutes have gone by and, except for that first sentence, everything you need is inside that dictionary in your left hand. I swear to you that the power of those thousands of words is infinite.

Now follow your instincts and imagine that you are Golem himself, a man or woman of letters. Those letters that compose you, exploding sympathetically like kegs of dynamite, shall choose their counterparts inside the dictionary. A few more seconds have ticked by but you still haven't used up even half your time.

And suddenly, like a shooting star, the first word awakes from its slumber and comes to you, lies down within you, humble, waiting. You must transcribe that first word, that short word that has grown and grown on its journey: VEIL.

This new word awakens all the others and the dictionary becomes restless. Before long, a second word comes to you: HANDS.

As if opening a surprise, pull on the end of the string and say hello to the sentence that comes packaged in parentheses: —(Yes, I put this veil over my face the day I burned my hands.)

And now three minutes have passed. By the time you write down the first sentence, several others come to you willy-nilly like moths to a flame, make a choice, and after thinking about it, open the second parenthetical package: —(People pitied me, especially because they thought I had also burned my face; and because of my secret, it seemed to me that I was above their false pity.)

You still have about two minutes. You don't need the dictionary anymore, put it down.

—(You know that I was a very beautiful woman and a dozen men used to send me flowers.)

The fourth sentence comes to you, as if chained to the heels of the third. —(One of those men burned his own face to put himself in my situation, he sent me a letter, now we're the same, you and I, he said in the letter, take this action as proof of my love.)

The last minute begins to slip away as the next to last sentence comes to you: —(I cried all night long, comparing my pride with my lover's insane humility; I thought that I should burn my own face.)

You must finish the last sentence in twenty-five seconds: —(It was not the physical suffering that held me back, but rather the thought that a love born of such a beautiful beginning would necessarily have a much more mundane continuation. On the other hand, I could not allow my lover to know my secret, I couldn't be that cruel. So I went to his house. He was also wearing a veil. I offered him my breasts, and we made love under the secrecy of the veil. And afterward, weeping, I plunged the knife into his heart. Weeping, because my innocent trick had proven so deadly.)

And you close the parenthesis, the end of the story, at the moment the last grain of sand in the hourglass falls.

MIKEL HERNÁNDEZ

ABAITUA

(b. 1959)

Abaitua is a professor at the Institute of Basque Language and Literature. After several contributions to magazines published in the Basque Country, he won the Ciudad de San Sebastián story competition (1980). His genre is the short story, and he is known for his collections, Panpin erreinua (The Doll Kingdom), published in 1983, and Ispiluak (Mirrors), published in 1985.

The story presented here, "Pedro Mainieri," is the last one in his book Ispiluak and falls under the section entitled "Munduaren ispiluak" (Mirrors of the World). The author employs a mirror technique in this story, in which the diary and the life of the protagonist each reflect the other.

Pedro Mainieri

*I am a man of letters. I feel through it, because of it, in rapport with it,
and with it I feel more.*
Gustave Flaubert

*I have never managed to see myself from the outside. There is no mirror that shows
us how we look to others, because there is no mirror that pulls us outside ourselves.
Another soul would be needed, another location for sight and thought.*
Fernando Pessoa

I. *A few pages from the diary of
amateur melodramatist Pedro Mainieri*

DECEMBER 2

I know Marta won't like it, but today I accepted an assignment to write
another soap for radio. As if I didn't have enough to do translating
novels! And she's against it, bitten by jealousy, as if my writing were the
enemy of our love. I remember what the Argonauts said, navigation is
necessary but life isn't. Maybe something like that happens to me, as
Bernardo said, sometimes life isn't necessary, but writing is. And I recall another saying, this one by Rilke, if you had to give up writing and
were able to live without it, then you shouldn't write another word.
I know one shouldn't write because it's fashionable, but my case is
none other than that. I am a "man of letters," as Flaubert said, a clumsy
imperfect man of letters, a humble writer of radio soaps, but it's necessary to me. Marta tells me I write more than I need to in order to live,
by which she means the less I write the more we could be together.
Why are we humans so possessive?

Reality fades away because I forget everything. And I can't bear to
see the way my past personalities and experiences are erased, how

things I've seen or learned are blotted out, how something I learned at one point leaves me while I'm learning something else: that nothing is definite in this frail, unbearable passing cloud of life; something within me reveals itself, I'm not satisfied and, like a child, I keep thinking I can do something about the forgetting. It would be better if memory were an inescapable repository. But it's full of holes. Memory is a strongbox full of holes in a town with no welders, and we are constantly wanting to fill it up, that it may never be completely empty.

DECEMBER 3

Marta told me to marry her. I told her no. I felt an irrational fear in my belly, as if there were an abyss within me, and I've come to the old apartment as an escape.

DECEMBER 4

Yesterday she was knocking at the door, but I didn't want to open it for her. And she will not come to this other house. Have I ever felt more pleasure in love than I have with writing or reading? After close examination, no. Writing is more calming, more peaceful, it doesn't betray you. It doesn't present you with problems. Difficulty, yes, but not problems.

DECEMBER 6

Marta has been calling and calling on the phone, but I haven't answered. It might be someone else, but I don't think so, because only she knows I've moved here, she would figure it out. How long has it been since I've been in this apartment? It belongs to the bank and my parents have been paying almost nothing for it. I don't know why the people at the bank haven't discovered that no one is living here. I remember we used to come here in the summer just for a change from the city, and then, too, because it doesn't get as hot here.

DECEMBER 8

I've come back to my own house again. I couldn't stand the telephone ringing all day, without a break.

DECEMBER 9

I've looked back over the entries I've written and realize that I haven't talked about anything but Marta and me. Not the work I'm doing or anything else. I need Marta more than I thought. This has happened to me before many times. I think I'm self-sufficient. I look in the mirror and I'm pleased with the company of my reflected image. I look in the mirror and I'm not alone. There are two people in the room.

DECEMBER 11

Yesterday no one called. I'm surprised. I'm fed up with being alone. At this moment I hate writing. Sometimes it seems I'm with Marta too much. I run away, thinking she's stealing my time, but after a few days of writing I'm satiated and it disgusts me. If she doesn't call today, I'll call her tomorrow.

Later. The older I get the faster time passes for me, and I feel dizzy. The days fly by, and that scares me. It seems like time is slipping through my fingers. Then time seems so precious to me that nothing else seems worth the trouble and I always go looking for something basic, something important for which to use this precious time. But there isn't anything.

II. *A few moments from the life of Pedro Mainieri*

DECEMBER 13
10:00 A.M.

The bed sheets and blankets were soft, so soft, when the phone rang, startling Pedro Mainieri awake. He thought it was Marta. Because of that he felt powerful, satisfied, because he was in charge. She can't live without me, he thought. Being awakened didn't bother him.

He took the phone in his left hand. "Yes?"

They were calling from the radio station to see what was happening with the first episodes of the soap.

He felt frustrated because he was sure it would be Marta calling him away from his work. Thinking about Marta, he started breakfast. He took a match, lit the stove, and put the milk on the burner to warm. Then he went to find his robe, a plush blue burnoose. The cold December air penetrated every corner.

He took sliced bread from its wrapper and put it in the toaster, still thinking about Marta. Why hadn't he heard from her? Could she really be tired of calling? She had never wearied of it so quickly before. What if she had tired of him for good? For a moment he thought about which would be better, putting up with Marta every day or putting up with the need for Marta that he was feeling in payment for not wanting to live with her.

5:00 P.M.

"It's fine," said the station director, the script in his hand. "Cigarette?"

"Sure." Pedro Mainieri extended one hand to take the offered American Winston and with the other pulled a lighter from his pocket to give the director a light. It seemed he wanted to talk.

"So, where've you been? They called from your fiancée's house more than once. I'm really sorry."

Pedro Mainieri suddenly stood up, muttered good-bye, and exited abruptly, leaving his Winston in the ashtray. The director was surprised. He's always been a strange sort, he thought, taking a deep drag on his cigarette.

Pedro Mainieri didn't know why he left the director's office so suddenly. He just had to. Why would he say, I'm sorry? He needed to get out of there and call Marta's house. She would surely be home. Although her afternoons were free, she didn't normally go out. For the first time it had turned out badly. He would have to call her in the end. It was always Marta who needed him the most and went looking for him. He felt conquered, beaten. Surely this time I've gone too far, he thought. And for the first time in a long time he was afraid of losing Marta.

In the street he went into the first phone booth he found and started dialing Marta's number: 814205. A thousand unconscious images passed through his mind as he dialed, as if the numbers themselves were trance-inducing. He stared into the distance, through the glass, toward a grove of trees, and with his gaze fixed on the trees he heard a voice on the phone.

"Hello?"

"Is Marta there?"

(Silence, confusion.) "Who is this?" (Marta's mother's voice.)

"It's Pedro." (Silence again, a painful nervous silence, and the voice answers uncertainly.)

"But Pedro, where have you been?" (A pause, as if wondering whether to continue speaking.) "Marta is dead, Pedro. We called every-where looking for you." (Another moment of silence.) "We buried her yesterday." (The voice fades.)

KOLDO IZAGIRRE

(b. 1953)

Izagirre has published works in different genres, including poetry, the short story, and the novel. His poem "Oinaze zaharrera" (To the Old Evil) was published in 1976. A book of short stories entitled Gauzetan (About Things) was published in 1979, and Euzkadi merezi zuten (They Deserved Euzkadi), a short novel excerpted here, was published in 1984.

Regardless of the genre, Izagirre demonstrates a constant preoccupation with language. In his 1977 book Zergatik bai (Why Yes?), a linguistic treatise inspired more by literary sensitivity than a normative spirit, there breathes a desire to flee from the grammatical trappings that ensnared the literary production of that time. This continuing desire to experiment with the language led him to incorporate different dialects and colloquial expressions in his 1981 book Euskal lokuzioak (Basque Idioms). In Euzkadi merezi zuten, Izagirre reconstructs stages of the social, political, and cultural past of the Basque Country, and through his efforts to balance academic and colloquial speech, he continues to experiment with the language.

The following excerpt is a chapter from the short novel mentioned above. It is undoubtedly realism, but with heavy poetic overtones that originate in the gentle irony used by the author when presenting places, characters, and situations. Also important is Izagirre's search for a new narrative language through his use of lexicon and syntax.

They Deserved Euzkadi

He had day-shift duty on Tuesdays and had to be there. News came that in Hernani they had been closed down since morning, they called Ereinotzu, but nobody knew anything there, it was possible that some had, they said. It wasn't yet nine o'clock when they heard the music. "Here they are!" said the foreman, "The Marseillaise!" and they went out to the bridge. Down the road came a brass band, a group of workers marching along behind. It looked like Holy Week, like when Hernani residents made a mock procession with whores up to the cider tavern of Ergobia, a flayed lamb carried on two boards, sausages hanging from sticks, and long loaves of bread for candles. They carried the Spanish tricolor flag. "Muera el rey!"[1] a woman yelled over and over again.

They paraded past the station toward the cider taverns. They were at the door. "Viva la república obrera!"[2] they shouted with fists raised. The manager closed up. The tram to San Sebastián left, full of people.

Basque farmers watched them with suspicion. "The Republic!" Hernani residents shouted at them, "The Republic!" They didn't need to knock on many doors. The taverns in Pagua, Otaño, Garratxena, Gurutzeta, and Oiharbide were soon filled with shouting. The Republic's proud flag stood on a pile of ferns.

They asked for silence, they couldn't hear him very well, and they asked him to start over. Then they lifted Indalecio Prieto onto a table, under the light bulb, a glass in his hand. When all the murmuring stopped, he repeated, "Workers! Before laws were made, kings ruled!" He waited for his audience to quiet down. He waved his arms clumsily, "And that's why they say there's no law that can dethrone a king!" The audience thought he would smash his glass against a cask. "Listen!" he said to them, holding it against his ear instead. The beads of sweat

---

[1] Death to the King!
[2] Long live the workers' republic!

on Prieto's face looked like wax dripping from an Easter candle in the Hernani church. "Listen!" and as even the sloshing in the cask quieted, he murmured, "Esa campana que se oye es la campana del Kremlin!"[3] and leaned toward the surprised faces of his audience. "Viva Rusia!" he shouted, and straightened so suddenly he struck the light bulb.

Neither on the job, where he extended the railroad from the dock, nor at home, where bread dipped in wine was his favorite dessert, did he speak a word. He was a man accustomed to hardship, he had become a total homebody. His words came like water from an eye-dropper. He had been a sheepherder in the Pampas. Claudia had remained in Buenos Aires, working as a maid. Once every three months they went to Santa Rosa. He would learn to drink mate. Some Indians were raffling off a mare at the fair, and he got lucky. He was happily leading it back to the ranch when it reared up, he couldn't handle it, surprised by a snake or something, and it ran off, dragging its bridle rope in the dust. Later he would see the Indians raffling off another horse, and it seemed to him it was the same one that ran away from him.

He had spent twelve years in America and six months in Amara. He paid for his return passage by working as a stoker on the steamship. He was a grateful man, a docile man, but he carried his head down in silence, stubborn, without murmuring so much as the blessing before a meal, and every Sunday when María hinted at breakfast that he should go to mass, he would get up from the table and go out into the garden. On the Sunday after his arrival, Father Matthew gave a sermon about the prodigal son, "Our brother, whom we thought dead, has come home, he who was lost has come back to life, and has appeared among us!" but Inazio Errazkin "wouldn't look to the church to see what time it was!"

Since the night before the town had been buzzing with the news that they were going to mobilize, and he headed for downtown San Sebastián. Soldiers were on patrol, people hurried by. In San Ignacio station a tram lay on its side like a cow struck down by dysentery. He heard they stopped Luzuriaga at gunpoint, in Pasaia, that they were ordering home Galicians detained on the picket lines. He heard they

[3] That bell that you hear is the bell of the Kremlin!

THEY DESERVED EUZKADI : 59

wanted to sack San Sebastián. Few shops and bars were open. The incident at Trintxerpe was ghastly.

wanted to sack San Sebastián. Few shops and bars were open. The incident at Trintxerpe was ghastly.

In Ategorrieta there were people at the windows. He headed out, ahead of time, fearful, the neighing of horses and the sound of their hooves, a dozen horse soldiers and a foot patrol. He passed by without even looking, careful not to quicken his pace, tense. "Halt!" He stopped, not knowing if he should turn around. The trees on Miracruz Street were as tense as he was. "Arriba las manos!"[4] said the voice of a pair of hands that pressed a gun to his back, "What have you got there?" said the voice insolently, ready to fire. "Drop it!" The lunch pail struck the sidewalk with the clunk of any empty container. Nervous hands loaded a bullet into the chamber, and a rough voice said, "Open it!" He bent down slowly, untied the knot. The rifle pressed against the nape of his neck. "Keep going!" They laughed at him, they wouldn't fire yet, "He's pissed his pants!", he was so afraid. Yelling was heard. He turned his head to look.

They came from Bidebieta, women and children in front, bold, fearless, they had broken through the police cordon and were coming down the street. They filled the street from one side to the other, Trintxerpe must have been emptied when they came. "We don't need spectators," said Zabaleta, taking his arm. "But the mounted police are in Ategorrieta!" he announced in surprise, but Zabaleta did not release his arm, "Individually we are nothing, united we are the people!" They moved up the street, and before he knew it, he was surrounded by bodies and shouting.

The captain moved to his troops, the union leader to the demonstrators. "Dice que teñen ordes de non deixarnos pasar!"[5] The captain spoke to the guards as well. No one moved. "Forward!" cried a woman, turning to the crowd. "A república é nosa, non deles!"[6] They advanced slowly, silently. There were people at the windows in Ategorrieta. A trumpet sounded. They were twenty meters from the Guardia Civil. The trumpet sounded, then a volley of shots, nobody moved. "Forward!" cried the union leader. The guards had shot into the air. They moved toward the guns to the sounds of shouting and hooves striking pavement, the guns were now pointed at the people.

[4] Put your hands up!
[5] He says he has orders not to let us pass.
[6] The republic is ours, not theirs.

When the trumpet sounded again, they fired the guns, the shouts became wailing, children before smoking guns, between stamping horses, brains spattered on trees like spit. "They belonged to someone, too!" Fleeing horses frightened the people, he saw it, they trampled the fallen. One man escaped by scrambling up Mt. Ulia, his empty sleeve flapping in the wind like an old flag. Hunched behind a tree, he saw the open door. The captain ordered the wounded to be placed in the truck, the weeping women came looking for their husbands. The door was open, he reached it in a breath. It would be better to go upstairs, an old woman stopped him on the first landing. "Assassins, that's what they are, those wild pigs!" The Guardia Civil in the street asked for mattresses to transport the wounded. Someone groaned in the doorway, they went down, he was leaning on the bannister, cursing, at the end of a trail of blood that led from the doorway. Afraid they would follow the trail of blood, the old woman went looking for the door key. He undid the napkin that wrapped his lunch box, the man's leg was badly injured, he didn't tie it too tightly. When the old lady locked the door, she murmured "I want nothing to do with those pigs!", but the man cut her off in midsentence with a pistol he pulled from his belt, "Abóa, gárdeme iste cachafullo!"[7] The old woman took it silently and told them to go upstairs. He squatted to retrieve his lunch box, then stayed there, staring at the tiny hole in the bottom of it.

There was an old saying that the people of Goizueta never fail. People at headquarters had warned them that after three days of rain the water would roar down the Urumea river. The stars moved in a crazy pattern, the rumbling of those black clouds would bring nothing good. The hurricane hit "on the day of Corpus Christi!"

Torrents of water came down Mt. Jaizkibel, uprooting trees, covering bridges, giant spools and pine logs from the Rentería paper mill filling the canal along with wood from the saw mill, like dead porpoises floating belly up. "Such a river, and no water in the house!" The ground began to open up and the people were afraid (many thought it was punishment from God), many cattle must have been lost.

On Saturday the assistant mayor came to their house to tell them they had to leave, everyone living on the side of the mountain had to

[7] Keep this for me, old woman.

move to high ground as soon as possible. They gathered a few clothes in the dark, they took some tools and that little winding motor. They weren't angry with the assistant mayor's order, "It's no use trying to hold back flood waters!", in the cellar the water was knee deep and it rushed down the slope of the garden clear to the chicken coop. In the schools they had placed mattresses for the evacuees. They turned the dog loose. Their sister told them to wait, she'd be back soon, and turned back to the house, she couldn't get her wooden shoes out of the mud, she went on with a sack, on to the chicken coop and barely made it inside before the wall collapsed destroying the cages, and the roof collapsed like a rockslide loosened by a blast.

ANGEL LERTXUNDI

(b. 1948)

Angel Lertxundi has published several works and is currently a professor of literature in the Escuela de Magisterio in San Sebastián. His first book of short stories, Hunik arrats artean (In the Senseless Afternoon), was published in 1971. It demonstrated a neorealist influence and a taste for the Latin American style of storytelling, a preference that became even more evident in his first novel, Ajea du Urturik (Something's Wrong with Urturi), published in 1977.

Lertxundi is the author of many children's tales and has attempted to recreate the traditional Basque story in his 1983 work Hamaseigarrenean aidanez (The Sixteenth Time's the Charm), winner of the Yon Mirande Basque government prize. He has also dedicated himself to seeking out a new aesthetic quality in popular language and expressions coined by the bertsolariak, or Basque troubadours. His literature explores the changes occurring in the Basque identity and utilizes forms and content that touch the collective unconscious of Basque society.

Urtero da aurten (Every Year Is This Year) was published in 1984. It is difficult to assign it a genre, for it is composed of brief passages of text that run the gamut from terse and witty reflections to short stories. Perhaps it could be called a series of humorous Basque personal impressions.

The excerpt presented here is a demonstration of the author's mastery of narrative language and of the timing necessary to a short story.

This Cold Earth Is Not Santo Domingo

By the time they buried me, the tired wrinkles on their faces, their imperceptible, deliberately shed tears, and their soft fleeting sighs had disappeared.

If you had been there you would have seen how Enkarni played with her skirt while the priest prayed. It was as if she wanted to protect it from a nonexistent south wind, or free it from an attack out of nowhere, looking for a reason to stare at my husband, everything in its place and hidden loves revealed, in public, among the continuous darting of teary eyes, waiting, seeking, looking, and praying, amen!, all their mouths opened, and I noticed a gold tooth in Enkarni's.

"Amen!" as if saying that small word required showing the gold tooth, she went to my husband and took his hand in hers, who knows what she said to him, "I'm sorry" or "I'm glad," naturally I was in no position to do more than read gestures, furthermore in situations like that people speak in whispers, not because we will hear them of course, an unexpected flapping of wings and a lapwing flutters by and circles the group, surprise and indecision on the bowed faces of the people, Enkarni's breast heaves as if she were startled by the bursting of an invisible balloon, and only when the bird disappears in the purple sky does she release my husband's hand, but he pays no attention to her, his gaze is directed at Jose, even though he has to crane his neck to see him, as if watching a soccer match from the cheapest seats, but Jose does not acknowledge him, doesn't look at him, he was standing discreetly in back of the crowd, not like that slut Enkarni, it's easy to see the difference, like when Jose said "you must take your wife to Santo Domingo," my husband ignored him, he aimed a glare as sharp as an acupuncture needle at him and replied stingingly, "Who asked you to bring a candle to this wake?" and actually my husband had no right to respond that way, Jose had offered me not only the candle but the fire to light it with, offered it, gave it, and tested it, of course my husband never knew what happened, but he always suspected something, otherwise why would he be craning his neck to get a look at Jose, but Jose was at the back of the group, and it wasn't polite for my husband to spend the whole ceremony straining for a look at him.

It must have been about ten years ago when my husband first began looking ridiculous to me, he would kiss me, with his bristly moustache, "do you like it?" and I had to say yes, what else could I do, but it scratched me and even disgusted me, especially after he ate, then I realized what was happening after I noticed how the phone bills were going up, the secret calls, I told Jose either the moustache goes or I do, he gave in, he thought he fooled me, both the moustache and the telephone at the same time, but one thing was certain, two years after I found out about Enkarni I took up with Jose, on my own initiative, on purpose, not for physical satisfaction at all, I was used to doing without, it was a game, a desire to do the same to my husband, and I'm sure I won, although speaking in this way from such a place certainly has its share of irony, to hell with that slut Enkarni, and I'm not saying that now because my husband didn't take me to Santo Domingo, not at all, my reasons started long before, almost right after we were married, my husband knew about my lung problem as well as I did, but he insisted on buying a house by the sea, and I had to breathe all the sea winds from Galicia and from the North, take them into my lungs and make them a part of me, until every breath felt like a rope tightening around my chest.

My blasted husband choked the life out of me by failing in his duty, my eyes were often wet with tears of hopelessness, a lot of time can pass before you're aware of it, until one day you look at yourself in the mirror and don't recognize what you see, who the hell are you?, the answer frightens you, there are dark puffy bags under your eyes, and that night for the first time your heart wins the battle against sleep, I decided to quit wasting my time, and I left the shabby hotel that was my life and went out into the world, I had no one but Jose, I myself had closed the door to any possibility between us, when you're young words like "adultery" pierce your heart like a knife, and later when you learn what they mean, you realize that the knife is still there, at first our relationship was superficial, I could not overcome my anxiety, poor Jose went away without a harsh word, I suffered a lot, I think he suffered, too, and when I saw in the mirror that I had no one but Jose, I went out after calling him on the phone, and he said,

"Daydreaming?"

I was waiting for him in front of a store window, watching people who meant nothing to me pass by in the glass, and he said again,

"Are you daydreaming?"

And I said, "It's something to do. How are you?"

We hadn't seen each other in two years, his expression was more somber, but as for the rest he looked as handsome as ever, his powerful shoulders could protect my dreams, my desire to live, and Jose said,

"Let's catch up on the last two years over a cup of coffee."

"Is there anything worth telling?"

A sympathetic smile.

"Have things been that bad for you?"

"Just life in general."

"You moved again, didn't you?"

We were sitting in a bar and I answered him, and as I did so, I began to cough, my lungs rebelled violently, Jose seized my elbows, two years before it might have been out of desire, out of a need to satisfy my sensuality, but Jose put his arm around my shoulders and I felt something stronger than compassion in the weight of his arm.

"What's wrong? You're not well."

Two years without seeing each other, without exploring each other's desire, and we had to meet like that, I was angry with myself, but it was useless, my cough grew drier and drier, he ordered me a camomile tea, and said,

"You're not at all well."

He asked me about my husband and I asked him not to mention him, but Jose was adamant:

"Yes, I must speak to your husband."

He went to a telephone, I begged him not to do it, he ignored me, dialed the number I reluctantly gave him, and said,

"Think what you want, but come as soon as possible. Your wife is not at all well."

I could not stop coughing, it was impossible to breathe, my life, my world, the bar were all suffocating in the short passage between my throat and my lungs, I don't remember anything, twenty days between white sheets in a hospital, my husband didn't tell anyone where he took me and I had no visits but his, as brief as they were boring, twenty days and he took me home again, to the seaside, to breathe in and swallow all the winds from Galicia, from the North, and all points on the compass. Jose was brave enough to come to the house and say,

"You have to take her to Santo Domingo."

My husband seized his arm and dragged him to the door.

"Who asked you to bring a candle to this wake?"

I don't know if my husband said these words or if I imagined them, it's been three long months since then, and now here, this is the first time I've seen Jose since, there at the back of the crowd, I don't need to stretch my neck, "Let's catch up on the last two years over a cup of coffee," but we couldn't have that cup of coffee, Jose, I asked you if there was anything worth telling, and of course there was, but when Enkarni saves her ridiculous skirt from the attack of an invisible wind, my husband will look at her, the priest will toss a handful of dirt on me, and it'll be over, I'll never breathe the sea air again, Jose, and as sure as there's a God, this cold earth is not Santo Domingo!

LAURA MINTEGI

(b. 1955)

Mintegi studied history at the University of Deusto and was published in various Basque periodicals. The collection of short stories Ilusioaren ordaina (The Cost of Illusion), 1983, was her first major contribution to Basque literature. The first story, "Satorzuloa" (Mole Hole) combines fantasy and reality in a historical setting. In spite of being the early product of a new writer, the story demonstrates a deep-seated ability to tell a story, both in form and theme. The combination of fantasy and reality gives "Mole Hole" a poetic quality.

Mole Hole

Raising her golden scepter, the queen ordered the brave young captive mouse brought before her, and the princess's heart beat so fast it seemed it would leap from her chest. The throne room was filled with silence. When the guards tossed the young prince at the queen's feet, a long "ooooh!" rose from the throats of all the mice. The prince was so handsome and graceful!

But he was a prisoner of the cruel war and, moreover, the son of the enemy king. The princess did not understand about armies or war. She didn't know why the mouse she loved had been thrown to the ground, and her eyes filled with tears.

No, this is no good. The prince should appear proud and haughty so that the court that captured him will be aware of the insult they've done him. Furthermore, when his father's army comes looking for him, he will legally take command and he must maintain his image as a leader at all times. Later will come the explanation of how they get married, and of how the two kingdoms were always attacking each other, and of how they are joined through marriage. Finally, the fruit of their union, a son, shall combine his mother's beauty with his father's daring.

Perhaps the story should take off from there. But what time is it? No wonder I was hungry! What do we have for lunch today? Leeks, potatoes, and fish! Fish makes everything better! Bread is not as black as it used to be, and I drink a glass of wine every day at lunchtime. Karmen, what kind of fish do you have there? Mackerel! Not bad. This morning I gave the story a big boost, but I won't write anything in the afternoon. I want to finish the illustration of the prince before the queen's court, his clothes torn and bloodied . . . the throne room is full of subjects . . . Who's knocking on the door? Go, go up! Shut the door and fasten the padlock!

The door is closed. On the wooden staircase in the light of a low-watt bulb, the cellar is left in a fog of darkness. Under the light of a folding lamp, the shine of a nearly bald head, and the silhouette of a receding chin and strong nose is visible against the darkness of the wall. On the table, pens and paper, a blue inkwell, black pencils and colored pencils, and a bunch of illustrated children's stories. In the corner, a bed eighty centimeters wide, and on it, clean sheets and a feather pillow in a pillowcase with the hand-embroidered initials "I. M." Over this, a white crocheted bedspread.

In the middle of the room, a dark table, flanked by two folding chairs and a small table lamp. Behind a blue-flowered cloth that served as a curtain were a sink, toilet, half bathtub, and small mirror with the silver backing showing at the corners. On a shelf under the mirror, a shaving kit, including an old brush, a comb and a toothbrush, soap, and lastly, fingernail clippers.

At both sides of the curtain a long white cloth was hanging as if to dry. To the right of the stairs, an armoire with a center door higher than its two side ones.

Footsteps are heard on the floor above. Who can it be? They hadn't had any unknown visitors in a long time and the ones they knew notified them ahead of time: Karmen's sister on Thursdays and Saturdays, to knit or have a snack; and her daughter, when it was necessary to help with the housework or to go to the city to do some shopping.

They hardly had any friends. Since '36, they had lost track of everyone; that was the best that could be said. The fate of others was known well enough. Dead in Madrid and Ebro-Santander. Nineteen thirty-seven was the hardest, when the final decision had to be made. The town was searched, the whole city council was shot, and all the young men dead, imprisoned, fled to the mountains, or God knows where. (He would certainly know their whereabouts.)

That wasn't the worst of it, no. Lost, we lost. No help from outside and inside a lack of organization, guns, leadership. We were born to lose. We had the onus of their Victory sign engraved on our foreheads from the first day. The horns were lowered and the summit unreachable. On the front lines when the Black Lady called us to the kingdom of darkness with winking and trickery, we knew there was no Victory sign in the trenches.

But who could be upstairs? Who is with Karmen? Those years, stained with the blood of youth, are revived for me in nightmares.

Karmen isn't coming, and I hear nothing upstairs.

Those years, soiled with poverty and decay. Dununciations every-where, and our women displayed on ox carts, their bare heads covered with tar. Karmen, the mayor's wife. Karmen on the ox cart, under the evil red eye of the denouncer. Days filled with filthy insults and humiliation. And her prince, in the mountains; a prince without a kingdom, a leader without an army.

I haven't heard anything upstairs in a long time.

But every dragon has its prince, and every prince his princess, and they have a white, winged horse that flies over problems and enemies to the kingdom of happiness. Without warning the prince's invincible sword blinds their enemies with reflected sunshine and the light of truth. That very sword will free the princess, seated silently in the court on her velvet throne, watching everyone, all of them gaping at her beauty.

Surely it's the neighbors. When the hell will that couple leave us in peace? When Karmen is out, they hear the faucet running; Karmen must have mice, because on many evenings they hear squeaking noises coming from the house; whenever she likes she should come to their house for a visit because living alone is not good for a woman . . .

Being alone, noises, faucets, neighborhood enemies. Such things do not exist in the kingdom of light. Neither do ration books. There is no black bread and no hunger. There's no fear either.

Fear, fear of noises. Fear of unusual silences. Barely visible behind the fog, the sun fell lower and lower, as if to keep the short winter days from lasting too long. A few street lamps lit up, and the gray humanity coming home from work formed a silent river whose water never changes. The capricious border between day and night danced about. Light and dark were friends, walking hand in hand . . .

In the cellar, the latter predominated. The dark cellar had not known sunlight since 1939. Since that time the brick-covered windows had not fulfilled their function of allowing light and fresh air to enter.

After throwing out all the old trash, we furnished this cellar, a place we wanted to make livable down through the years. A mole cellar. A mole hole.

On the floor in one corner are piled paper and documents on official letterhead. Next to that, letter files and municipal archive cards. On the other side, brightly colored pictures and sketches, white horses and fire-breathing dragons next to princesses dressed in gold cloth. Next to these, brave and loyal mouse princes, facing danger, not knowing the meaning of the word "fear."

Karmen hurried down to the cellar. She was carrying dessert and coffee. Someone who wanted to sell her an automatic vacuum cleaner kept her at the door for twenty minutes. When the salesman left, her sister arrived, out of breath. She had a newspaper under her arm: because the first of October was approaching, the Generalissimo had decided to grant an open amnesty, and many political prisoners would be freed: communists, reds, republicans, and anarchists.

The autocracy was loosening a bit, and upon hearing the news, many narrow-muzzled mustachioed mole leaders poked their blind eyes and earless heads into the light.

Karmen didn't have too much faith in it, but she had dreams of ending her double life, and this article gave them renewed strength. She tried to make the shiny-domed inhabitant of the cellar believe the good news.

Go out. To go out, after spending his adult life forgetting what sunshine is like. Into the world of real light. Go out. How can I go out into a world where dragons take on the appearance of men? Into a world without the blue-eyed, red-lipped princess? Verified, revealed to reality, and taken away from me; it would defile my dreams!

In the days that followed, after a long period of idleness, he engaged in furious bursts of activity that Karmen knew nothing about.

I will place wings behind the white horse's ribs. They must be long and finer at the tips, thrown back so they don't strike the hind legs. Long and ethereal, like the deeds he must achieve. I shall create long-legged, slender-bellied horses, like those El Greco would draw. This princess has very large feet. They must be finer, in the Japanese fashion. I'll shorten them a bit.

I don't think it's appropriate to have a dark princess. Her hair should be golden, to reflect the sunlight.

Karmen returned the cold, untouched dishes to the kitchen. Her husband wasn't tasting, or even smelling, the food. The daily newspapers, unopened, were piling up in the space under the stairs.

The cellar had taken on the unpleasant odor of a closed, stuffy space. Karmen, the good wife, preached useless sermons at him. The subject of amnesty was neither forbidden nor welcome; it was just ignored. The ghost of the imaginary princess filled every nook and cranny of the cellar, her light conquering the dark.

Karmen brought dinner. He wasn't there. Her question brought forth no answer from behind the curtain that concealed the toilet. He wasn't under the stairs, or under the bed either.

Beside the table, moving toward the circle of light defined by the folding lamp, she saw a reddish-brown mouse about twenty-five centimeters long, very proud and arrogant, with blind eyes and no ears.

A crown sparkled on its head, and next to its right front leg, a pencil hung like a sword.

The mole became a mouse, became a mole in the cellar.

RAMÓN SAIZARBITORIA

(b. 1944)

Saizarbitoria's name is associated with the modernization of the Basque novel both because of the themes he develops and his narrative style. His first novel, Egunero hasten delako (Because It Begins Every Day), published in 1969, offers a fresh approach by telling a story through action, temporal planes, and the use of different grammatical persons.

His second novel, 100 metro (100 Meters), was published in 1976 and relates the desperate attempt of a militant to escape the police before finally being shot down. The easily visualized structure made the book a natural for the screen, and it was produced by Basque Television in 1985 as part of a promotional program for Basque literature sponsored by the Basque government.

His third novel, Ene Jesus (My Jesus), published in 1979, introduces us to Samuel, suggestive of Beckett's character, living in a world turned fatally inward upon itself.

The text presented here is the last chapter of the book Ene Jesus. Here we see the continuous, circular monologue of the book, a story that never ends because it never really began, a story told and untold in the pages of the book. The style is noteworthy for its austerity, the result of a risky pruning of the language.

My Jesus

FINAL CHAPTER

It's a matter of lifting your right arm, placing it across your chest, then letting it drop to take hold of the left edge of the sheet. Take the edge of the sheet. Take the edge of the sheet and lift your arm. Hold it out to your right without dropping the end. The leg. Move your left leg away from your right one. Swing it across the bed until your knee is bent by its weight and your foot falls to the floor. Find the edge of the bed springs with your right arm. The cold bed springs.

To start with, throw off the sheets. Grasp the left edge of the sheet in your right hand and pull it to the right. With your right hand. First take them off your feet, throwing them up forcefully. Forcefully. Next pull the left edge toward the right. Your feet are free. Move your left leg. Move it by forcing it sideways, off the bed. Your foot's on the floor. Lift your body. To lift your body, first place your left hand on the edge of the bed springs. On the edge of the bed springs. To do this, lift your arm. First, move your arm. Extend it. It's not easy. The arm.

It's not worth the effort. Everything in its place. Sheets under the chin. Aluminum can on the floor. The mystery of its pull tab still a secret. The chiming of tower bells marking the unknown hour. My body's reflection in the ceiling mirror. Feet in the air so as not to obstruct my pedaling. "Around the world on wide roads," Samuel used to say. "In Maracaibo or Copacabana, stroking the generous thighs of those who offer interested red-painted smiles." Or "combing the blond hair of those who grow bored sitting on their high chairs." Anything that began with "once upon a time." "In the end, the possibility of forgetting this miserable existence and inventing another," he said once, lips covered with foam from his beer. But the moist eyes of the world did not believe it.

In spite of that, he said nothing.

He didn't believe it. The tower bells. The metallic resonance of the lost chord hanging in the air. The time. I don't finish anything I start. The agenda, recognizing the can, the time. Having to identify it in the colors of the light. The mist of green light that filtered through the leaves of those slender beech trees in the park. When he wounded her over and over—the perceived warmth of her blood. When he dominated her naked body. When he tied her up with the patterned dress I liked so much. "Do you want to see me?" she said. More likely, "Do you want to see me like this?" and a trail of blood trickled over the soft skin of one of her thighs.

"Do you want to see me like this?" she said to me, abandoned on the ground, wanting to cover her vanquished body by crossing her legs, and the echo of her voice joined the demented laughter of the other, that ventriloquist's laugh. And coming out from behind a stone wall I picked up the fallen weapon, and when I approached them, I saw them locked in an embrace, on the yellowing grass, alternating one body on top of the other, they were laughing, each trying to hide in the other's body. Their bodies, their laughter, their embraces, even their smells. I remember.

"You're late again today," he would say in the darkness of the room, seated on the edge of the bed, probably pulling a white handkerchief out of the sleeve of her black sweater. "Late." The metal edge of the bed springs in his throat.

And although I hear bells, I will keep my eyes shut, and I'll wait for the discordant noise to cease, and even though my eyes are closed, I'll be able to see the intense white light that will filter through my eyelids.

But in spite of everything, I won't open my eyelids until the end. Because it's not worth the effort. A can, and when it's picked up, another can to fill its empty spot, the iron bars that crisscross the window that leads nowhere. The mirror on the ceiling and my imagination reflected there.

And these toes that exude life even though they are immobile. With their own heart. As if they overflowed with life from their own heart. Waiting for the order to move.

But I will cross my hands on my chest and will not open my eyes. And you will dress me also like a Carmelite, Mother. Like Father. And you will cry, but I will not escape to Redox. And you will not have to scrub all the stairs in the world for me. And I won't come home late anymore, while you twist a white handkerchief in worry against your stomach.

That soft moist yellowing belly. I feel it vibrate against me in the echo of the words you always speak. The mystery of the warm moist belly when it divides in childbirth. You my-beloved-son, only-one-that-I-have-in-the-world, you, for whom I would give my life if it would make something of you. You, my only hope.

That's how Mother is.

And in the station there was no deaf-mute and no Samuel to tell stories to the ladies waiting for the train whose whistle sounded like the cry of a baby. And there was no station. And I could not get used to the corners in Turkish toilets. And everything was sand. Fine, dry sand. Powder. And there was only you to take care of me. You waited for me to go to bed, crossing your wrinkled hands over your soft, moist belly, squeezing a handkerchief.

This way, not that way. Don't go that way.

Seven, fourteen, twenty-one, twenty-eight, thirty-five, forty-two.

Thirty-two, forty-two, forty-nine, forty-nine, fifty-six.

Sixty-three, seventy, sixty-seven, seventy-seven, seventy-seven.

JOSEBA SARRIONAINDIA

(b. 1958)

Sarrionaindia entered the literary world with the people who gave life to the underground journal Pott. He has written numerous short stories that have won different literary prizes. For "Maggie indazu kamamila bat" (Maggie, Make Me Some Chamomile Tea) he won the Ignacio Aldekoa prize in 1984; for "Enperadore eroa" (The Crazy Emperor) he won the Ciudad de Bilbao prize, also in 1984; and for "Gizon gordelekuetan barrena" (In Human Hideaways) he won the Resurrección M ª de Azcue prize.

He is yet another writer experimenting with poetic language and the archetypes of universal literature. In his work we recognize the echo of various authors. His language is elitist and removed from the vernacular, all for the sake of greater precision, but he doesn't hesitate to make use of dialectical variations. In the past he has translated T. S. Eliot and Fernando Pessoa into Basque.

"Estazioko begiradak" (Glimpses of the Station) is the first story in the 1983 book Narrazioak. It is actually an exercise in the theory of fiction writing, a telling and untelling of numerous stories, inspired by a bare setting, an empty train station and a pair of chairs. This brief but important story is a testimony to Sarrionaindia's work.

Glimpses of the Station

An empty station, two chairs, and sadness can invent a thousand stories.
Michel Saulaie

The last train has passed, lost on the endless rails, and nothing is left but silence scented with old oil. On the outskirts of the city, night, with its dangerous dreams, falls irresistibly over a dilapidated train station. A dim light spreads, like a spider web, in timid strands from a single weak bulb. A wall clock with a broken crystal and unmoving hands watches over everything. A few withered purplish plants grow in tiny pockets of earth among the gray stones. There are also two chairs, half in shadow where the strands of light fade into darkness. And there is a woman seated on one of the chairs; she wears black shoes and a blue skirt, and the newspaper she holds open before her cannot hide her greenish shirt or sweater. If the switchman passed by, he would stop and look at her, feeling obscene desire or imagining who knows what, but during their time off the switchmen amble through the main streets of the city.

The woman on the chair, Marie Laure, is perhaps reading want ads, looking for work. She has left her parents and birthplace behind to come to the city. A girl like you, they said to her, will get lost wandering around here alone. She came to work as a maid, but she'll take any job. Her eyes no longer reflect goats or swallows or heads of wheat. Nor do they reflect colorful shop windows, the glow of traffic lights, or the faceless crowds of travelers. They have faded like figments of a dream, and the station has become an empty stage. Walking on sidewalks, they told her, is nothing like walking through wheat fields where the spikes of wheat caress your legs. It's more tiring. They gave her the address of a boardinghouse, but she keeps it in her pocket because she has already walked too much, and she will spend the night on this empty stage, taking counsel from the stars.

But no, that's not right, she's not reading the paper because there isn't enough light, she's just staring at it. Ana is the name of the woman on the chair, the wife of a famous architect, a lady who spent two years in an insane asylum. Her son went to war and died, and they say she went crazy, forsaking clothes, mirrors, and laughter. Alone, she talks to herself about childhood games, first kisses exchanged among white flowers, the pain of childbirth, how the baby looked just like his grandfather, the way he smiled at the age of four, and the moment the long crowded train carried him off, dressed like a soldier. Look, child, she says, here comes the train, chug-a-chug. Every evening she comes to this station and cries until a household servant comes looking for her. Let's go home, ma'am, she'll say, it's time to nurse the baby.

When she folds the paper and puts it in her purse, you can tell that she's younger. Her name might be Agatha, why not?, and perhaps she has just attended her father's funeral. Away from her family for a long time, the rebellious daughter of a proud, conceited father, she has just returned from viewing the corpse of the old army officer in his coffin. Last night, when the weeping relatives left, she took his medals off his body and replaced them with fake tin-plated ones. Then she took off her garter and placed it in the pocket of the corpse's old uniform as a gift from daughter to father. She kept a vigil over the body, sitting on the window ledge, until sunrise. After the afternoon funeral, she came to the dirty station to remember, or perhaps to forget, she doesn't know which. It's cold, tomorrow she'll head south.

It could even be a lady, Arantxa, who has come to wait for her husband. She has dirty black hair, a long face, stretched by the constant opening of her mouth, and in the darkness of her big round eyes there burns a pale flame. This is barely perceptible. Reaching toward her, the threads of light fade to nothing, and only a few pitiful lost rays manage to caress her. She exudes a sweet melancholy charm. There's no one around, for whom is the charm? For no one, and even so she waits. She believes her husband will arrive on the eleven o'clock train, she left the baby sleeping in its cradle, and she doesn't know that there is no eleven o'clock train.

Or let's suppose, with her bright-colored clothing, she's a whore, Claudine. She has whitened her cheeks with rice powder in order to cover her wrinkles. She's a dark shadow among the black butterflies of the night, waiting for a traveler, or perhaps just wanting to be alone. Life is exhausting, she thinks, on leaden afternoons. Hey, you—who's she talking to?—want to touch between my legs? Nothing but shadows around, train cars and dry plants, and her skin is without a buyer in this silent place. She has a small bottle of cognac in her purse among her creams and mascara. She takes it out and has a drink. Too many years have passed since she received her last love letter; as for writing one, she never has.

But no. It's not true. There is no woman on the chair, there's no one. It's all an illusion. Imagination created her and gave her life, formed her from nothing, and placed her on the chair. Yes, it was the imagination of the man sitting over there on the other chair that invented the woman when he wanted his eyes to meet someone else's across the lonely station. He's wearing a black hat and a dark blue jacket, all his clothes look black in this place. No feeling or desire shines in his face, as he gazes at the other chair, then at the palms of his hands. If the switchman's wife moved the edge of her curtain at home and looked through the window toward the station, she would know that he is not her husband, but she is busy in her kitchen, unaware.

It's Louis. His cousin was ten years old when they agreed, one starry night, to strip naked in front of each other in this station. The little girl undressed, taking her shirt off over her head and dropping her skirt, to reveal a slender pale body. The man in the station now remembering that event, a boy then, had run away without undressing, pleased with his trick and awed by the half-discovered mystery of her body. This afternoon, when he saw her cross the sidewalk, he saw resentment in his cousin's face just as he had that night.

Or he's a street sweeper, Joao Miguel; his suit fools no one, because it's so worn out. It's not time to go to work yet, he works the midnight to dawn shift, and he's waiting. He's thinking about the broken doll and the wheelless bicycle he must collect and burn. The stars are thumbtacks of light in the dome of heaven, and a cool breeze is blowing, but it will be colder at dawn, especially the hour before sunrise. They'll put on their yellow jumpsuits and go down every street in the city in their big yellow truck, collecting cardboard boxes from behind theater billboards, broken glasses from the front of the discotheques, and moth-eaten chairs from the square by the church. And now the street sweeper feels like an apple rotting slowly in its box in the fruit market.

On the other hand, it might be a lonely old man named Jon. You can see gray hair under his ridiculous hat. If he has any children, they are far away, like birds who have left the nest, too far away. The cherries are ripening on the other side of the world, but here there is only drought. Life is like peeling an onion, he says. It makes you cry a lot. Life is like a castle of sand, he says. It's worn down by the waves. His children have told him they will return. He's writing down a melancholy poem from memory about this station: like a watch crushed by train wheels a hundred times a day . . .

It's possible that he's a poet, but it's more likely that he's a journalist. He is Malcolm, a journalist. You must follow that girl, they told him last night, take some photographs and see where she goes and with whom, four pages worth. So like a detective, he spent his day shadowing the girl until he lost her trail and wound up in this peaceful place. Here he can drink from the little whisky bottle in his pocket. You take away my shakes, dear, he says to the bottle. Later he will have to take up the search for the girl again, from one pub to another, to see if he can get some good photos of her in an unguarded moment. Furthermore he'll have to see if she reserved any tickets at the airport. Maybe he'll get lucky and catch her with a lover. But things are never what you want them to be.

Or perhaps he is someone recently released from prison after serving twelve years. Thomas spent his childhood in this neighborhood, running around and playing pranks. Most likely he has a yellowed photograph in his pocket from those days that he can recall without even looking at it: he's six years old, wearing short pants, a shirt with vertical black stripes, carrying his hoop in one hand and his stick in the other; he remembers the photo and he bites his bottom lip. He has wandered through the city, looking for someone he knows, but he hasn't found anyone. And yet, nothing has changed in those twelve years. He smells the same scent of dahlias as before, even though there are no dahlias to be seen, no blue ones, or red ones, or white ones.

But no. It's not true. There is no man in the chair, there's nobody. It's all an illusion. Imagination gave birth to it all, creating the images from nothing, and placing them in that chair. Yes, the imagination of the woman who was seated nearby in the other chair invented the man when she wanted to meet another's eyes across the empty station. The last train went by some time ago to lose itself on the endless tracks, and almost nothing remains in the station, except a whiff of oil and thin threads of light from one bulb. A few ore cars, some sparse and scraggly plants, empty mail sacks against the dark walls, a big clock with no hands and no crystal, a black silent bell hanging from the canopy, and two old broken wooden chairs rotting in the silence, because silence never catches the train.

ARANTXA URRETAVIZCAYA

(b. 1947)

Urretavizcaya made her debut in Basque literature in 1971 with a collection of poems entitled San Pedro bezperaren ondokoak (After St. Peter's Eve) and ten years later in 1981 she published a second book of poems, Maitasunaren magalean (In the Lap of Love), winner of the Ciudad de Irún prize for poetry. However, her narrative works suggest a more personal presence and provide a more decisive contribution to the modern panorama of Basque literature. Her short novel Zergatik panpox (Why, Darling?), published in 1979, and her three stories in Aspaldian espero zaitudalako, ez nago zekula bakarrik (I'm Never Alone Because I've Been Waiting for You for So Long), published in 1983, are lyrical in style and intimate in tone. Zergatik panpox was made into a movie by the Basque government and Basque Television in 1985.

The excerpt presented here is a chapter from the short novel Zergatik panpox. This text is remarkable for its multiple voices, and the free combination of various discourses (mother to son, mother to departed lover, mother to self) which are dialogues in the form of monologues. The reader hears only the words of the protagonist narrator, but there is dialogue, nevertheless.

Why, Darling?

(EXCERPT)

Since Txema left, all I have to do is look at the color of Antxon's eyes to know what mood I'm in. Arise, sad and oppressed worker. In order for Antxon to sleep well, seven-eight-nine, abracadabra, I must be happy. When I feel empty and rotten inside, or when I feel nervous and aggressive, a mother without Txema, who has learned to recover but not to live, I must appear alive, peaceful, and calm for Antxon. Alley-oop, seven-eight-nine, everything Antxon touches comes to life, darling, mamma is tired today, but not sad. You have to take a bath tonight, that's certain. You have to show daddy how you're learning to swim. Mamma, just like in the swimming pool, and there's water splashed on the bathroom floor, mamma, I'll learn how by summertime, a puddle on the floor getting his slippers wet, mamma look, my head's under water. Softness, the smooth white skin of his bottom shining brighter than a diamond because of the water, skin that has never been in the sun. The puddle is going to get the rug wet, don't go, mamma, look how I'm swimming, mamma, I have to tell daddy that I learned to swim. What happens to children's fannies, when do little boys lose their bottoms, Txema had a fanny, I remember the warmth of it when I would crawl back in bed after getting up because Antxon was crying, Txema facing the wall, his knees pulled up, defending his sleep, because a man's sleep is too important to be disturbed by the cry of a child. The steam from the hot water is wetting my eyes and the tiles on the wall, it's better not to think about it, be careful, as if your head were sick, don't think, don't move. My darling's smooth bottom, mamma, giver of kisses. Come on, chubby, dry yourself off, dinner and off to bed. Okay, while you swim a little more, I'll make dinner, rice soup and fried fish, but if we're going to play at boxing you have to hurry, well, too bad if you ate fish earlier, too, there isn't anything else, well, okay, rice and eggs. To express a woman's love, when she's exhausted at the end of the day, take a picture of her making dinner, click, love repeated every night, omelettes, soup, and fruit salad.

Let's go, Antxon, the soup is done, come on, I'll dry you off because you'll never finish, who's that little blond darling in the mirror? Yes, I'll tell you a story at bedtime, yes, I'll give you hugs, and when will you give me hugs, when I call you to me during the night, at least my darling's sleep isn't sacred, at least you, my child, will know how to care for another's sleep. While you eat your soup, I'll fry the fish. Once upon a time, there was a fisherman in a little Basque village, and this fisherman caught a bib fish for Antxon, but Antxon didn't want to eat it. Okay, it's true, it's not a good story, but it would have been better if you had eaten the fish instead of the egg, you have to eat a lot of fish if you're going to grow up big and strong, blow on it a little if it's hot. Come on, go potty, brush your teeth, and get in bed, okay, we'll play boxing for a while, I'll have to do something if I want you to get over this afternoon's fright. Irritation, I had no reason for it. Mamma, I like to play boxing with you better than with daddy, sometimes daddy hurt me, when will daddy come get me at school. All right, off to bed, yes, I'll tell you a story like I promised, I didn't forget, but silly, I told you it was because of a road block, let's not start on that subject again, how was I going to forget to pick you up, how was I going to forget my best friend in the whole world, darling of my heart, next time you mustn't get so nervous, sit down on the curb and grandma and I will arrive soon. Once upon a time there was a little boy named Antxon the Lollipop Kid who had a smile so pleasant and so wide, it chased away the storm clouds, with soft peach fuzz on his face, golden eyelashes in front of calm sea-blue eyes, and hair the color of wheat, when you're bigger, my darling, you will work and I will rest, and if I'm thirsty at night you will bring me some water, and I won't cry when you're a little late picking me up. Once upon a time there was a little star named Antxon in my sky, a black sky with a single star, once upon a time, my right hand on your back while I rub it from the neck to the waist, once upon a time, there was a flower named My Darling, a sunflower no doubt, golden-haired, or perhaps a furze blossom growing on the edge of a cliff and you were my only support. Once upon a time, there was a little bird named Antxon and this bird was not the son of just any mamma bird but the son of a star. Once upon a time, sleep, little one, now my hand rubs from your bottom up, Antxon had a mother, sleep, my darling, the left hand moves softly, secretly, and his mother had a father, a brave warrior, a white knight fallen from the heavens, someone who does not lose sleep at night or after lunch over silly matters, quiet, quiet, daddy's sleeping, and mamma's hand, sleep, my darling, is on your neck, caressing your soft curls, she had dreams, dreams without an Antxon or a Txema. One night, when white flowers looked reddish-brown, the color of my father's Sunday shoes, if I stop my hand I can feel your heart beat, asleep from the waist up, a dancer's waist, it hasn't even reached your heart yet, on that day of red flowers, the sea behind the eyelids was completely calm, my darling, little sea snails, on that day there lived a mother without children and this mother believed that there was a road that led to happiness, happiness was a continent and the road to it was full of seas, and storms, and streams overflowing their banks, and this mother believed that the road to happiness was exhausting and heroic, very exhausting and not so heroic, and the keys that open the doors to the pleasures of the world could only be obtained with solid boring discipline, sweet, humble, fragile, perfumed and painted ladies, but at night they have to guard the man's sleep like a treasure, sleep, my child, don't cry, your father will wake up, miraculous women, who iron clothes at dawn, who always have something to clean when they are on the verge of falling asleep, sleep, my child, don't wake your father. So sleep, my darling, no, I'm sure I'll never be late again, that's why that mother wanted a little girl. Blood with shame and secrecy. If I stop my hand, I can feel sleep settling into your lungs, penetrating every corner. Once upon a time, there was a mother without a husband or a son, not because she had eyes and skin the color of the earth, but because she was the daughter of a stern father, and there was always a mountain of clothing to iron, a mountain of clothing between dreams and the sea. My hand on your shoulder, my darling, pushing sleep into your eyes and nose, spreading out from your lungs, the nose is the last part of my darling to fall asleep, there, sleep and wakefulness fight their last battle, trying to conquer the sides of your nose, my darling, my hand will not rest as long as your nose is moving. Before bringing a son into the world that mother had such a slender waist, she was a mother before she had a son. "Rockabye, baby in the treetop," your nose has calmed down. Why did Txema leave, my darling? The only truth is the peace and happiness in your face, from the waist up, from the neck to the head, I don't need anyone to guard your sleep. Why did Txema leave? It's best not to think about it, be careful, you'll get sick, I don't need anyone to put your nose to rest, my darling, my hand is enough, but why, why shouldn't the sick be moved? Ten, eleven, twelve, Antxon is asleep. Nine-fifteen. I'm drowning, my darling, the streams have overflowed their banks.